THE LAST COLONIAL

CURIOUS ADVENTURES
AND STORIES FROM A
VANISHING WORLD

THE LAST
COLONIAL

CURIOUS ADVENTURES
AND STORIES FROM A
VANISHING WORLD

CHRISTOPHER
ONDAATJE

Images by Ana Maria Pacheco

Thames & Hudson

First published in the United Kingdom in 2011 by
Thames & Hudson Ltd, 181A High Holborn, London WC1V 7QX

Copyright © 2011 Christopher Ondaatje

Introduction Copyright © 2011 Michael Holroyd

Images Copyright © 2011 Ana Maria Pacheco
courtesy of Pratt Contemporary

British Library Cataloguing-in-Publication Data
A catalogue record for this book is available from the British Library

ISBN 978-0-500-25186-7

Printed and bound in China by Toppan Leefung

To find out about all our publications, please visit www.thamesandhudson.com.
There you can subscribe to our e-newsletter, browse or download our current
catalogue, and buy any titles that are in print.

CONTENTS

ABOUT THE ARTIST

Christopher Ondaatje is a compelling writer and when I was asked to make images for his book, The Last Colonial, *it was a challenge. Both of us come from colonized countries but our narratives are not the same. However there is common ground: while Sri Lanka and Brazil have different histories and stories, in our youths we were exposed to one of the most enduring aspects of both cultures – the mythical world.*

We live in post-colonial times where changes and transformations occur very rapidly, so memories of the past should be preserved to give meaning to our lives. After all, we shall never cease to be fascinated by the mysteries of the human soul.

ANA MARIA PACHECO, 2011

THE BRILLIANT PAINTER, sculptor and printmaker Ana Maria Pacheco was born in Brazil in 1943, but has lived in England since 1973. Her work deals with issues of control and the exercise of power, drawing upon the tensions of the old world and the new. In 1996 she was invited to be the Artist in Residence at the National Gallery in London. She was the first non-European and the first sculptor to receive this honour, which she held until 2000.

She is best known for her multi-figure groups of sculptures carved from wood. These include *Man and His Sheep* (Birmingham Museum and Art Gallery), and *Dark Night of the Soul*, created during her residence at the National Gallery.

The images for *The Last Colonial* reveal an unusual understanding of some scarred and troubled experiences of the author.

ACKNOWLEDGMENTS

ALMOST TEN YEARS AGO, I went to Kenya and Tanzania and wrote a book on Ernest Hemingway in colonial Africa, focusing on his great short story, 'The Snows of Kilimanjaro'. Then I returned to my birthplace, Ceylon (which in 1972 had become Sri Lanka), and wrote another book on Leonard Woolf as a civil servant in colonial Ceylon, which drew upon Woolf's little-known but accomplished *Stories of the East*, published by his Hogarth Press.

Both Hemingway and Woolf based their short stories firmly on their own experiences, and this set me thinking. Even as a young boy I always wanted to tell and write stories, and the urge remained strong as an adult. But to write a good short story requires something to write about . . . some experience of life. Of course, mastery of the form requires more than such experience: Hemingway attained this mastery, unlike Woolf. Anyway, I found that I could not resist the challenge of trying to follow in their footsteps, however hesitantly. During the past decade, I put down recollections and stories ranging over seven decades since the 1940s, during which the colonial empires of my childhood vanished. Some stories are essentially autobiographical, others are invented, while the majority are a mixture of autobiography and invention. Yet all of them are inspired by true experiences – even the final, strange story about my house in Devon, 'The Glenthorne Cat'.

Along the way I made many mistakes, but I also gained many advisers and people who encouraged me. The short story form opened new doors for my writing. My friend and mentor John Fraser, Master of Massey College in Canada, who helped get my early books published, accused me of inventing the non-fiction short story. I wish I had. In England, Clive Aslet, then editor of *Country Life*, gave over eight uninterrupted pages of the magazine to 'The Glenthorne Cat', and thereafter published other pieces of mine. Andrew Robinson, while he was literary editor of the *Times Higher Education Supplement*, was particularly helpful and demanding in giving me assignments. The *Spectator* also gave me books to review, which sometimes became the germ of stories. In Sri Lanka, the *Nation* published a number of my post-colonial experiences. In Canada, *Books in Canada*, before its sad demise, and the *Literary Review of Canada* gave me various literary tasks and further encouragement. I am grateful to all of these editors and publications.

Michael Holroyd, an admired near-neighbour in Devon, deserves special thanks for agreeing to write the introduction. Ana Maria Pacheco was somehow intrigued enough by the stories to agree to produce images for them. These images are enigmatic and sometimes disturbing but, being a colonial herself – from Brazil, rather than Ceylon – she understood my obsessions. 'The devil drives.' For me, and I believe for many others, her interpretations of the stories have a touch of genius.

Finally, I am indebted to Michael Berry who helped me to assemble the many different components of *The Last Colonial*; and to Thames & Hudson, my publisher, for being so understanding and producing the book to their usual high standard.

Of all my books, this is the one that has given me the most satisfaction.

CHRISTOPHER ONDAATJE

For my mother
Enid Doris Gratiaen
who gave me confidence

INTRODUCTION

SIR CHRISTOPHER ONDAATJE is a man of many interests, talents and careers: an athlete, explorer, businessman, publisher, writer and patron of the arts. In Britain he has become celebrated chiefly for his patronage of the visual arts – in particular for his support of the Royal Society of Portrait Painters, the creation of a splendid new wing named after him at the National Portrait Gallery in London, and his original private museum and gallery on the northern Devon–Somerset border. But despite these achievements, it is literature I suspect that remains his favourite art (one of his beneficiaries has been the Royal Society of Literature, of which he is an honorary fellow).

This mosaic of essays, resembling non-fiction short stories, is probably the nearest we will get to reading a complete autobiography and it will be of considerable value to any future biographer. The book gives us glimpses of the author's early adult life in Canada (revealing his passion for jazz and a wonderful *Boy's Own* adventure as a member of the Canadian bobsledding team which won a gold medal at the Winter Olympics in 1964). There are vivid and dramatic sightings too from his childhood days in Ceylon which have imprinted themselves on his memory and imagination. We are also taken on his extensive travels, quests, explorations and discoveries – journeys which reveal the stories behind his full-length studies of Sir Richard Burton, Ernest Hemingway and Leonard Woolf, as well as his search for the source of the Nile and his famous book *The Man-Eater of Punanai*.

Non-fiction writers, we are told, tend to embellish or exaggerate their facts, slightly shifting time or place 'so as to make a narrative more evocative or more exciting for the reader'. Ondaatje does not indulge in such wayward devices, though he sometimes uses direct speech to make his effects more immediate. Essays and short stories have recently occupied an unjustly neglected corner of English literature. Many people have praised them, though few were to be seen reading them. But reading habits are changing – and changing fast. Those massive, well-regarded volumes of non-fiction scholarship which stood so proudly like galleons hugging the coast of Britain, as if defending her island culture from foreign vessels, have been becalmed and are retreating into harbour. In their place, moving with ease and elegance across the waves with the trade winds filling their sails, are fleets of smaller craft: fantastical and historical fictions, experimental hybrids and speculative non-fictions which travel with speed and ingenuity and are welcomed by other countries. We are less insular than we were.

In his Prologue, Ondaatje tells us of the 'carefree wilderness' of his childhood in Ceylon and how it was brutally followed by the unkind and gratuitous discipline of Blundell's, the English public school to which he was sent in 1947 at the age of thirteen in the expectation of him being turned into an Englishman. In 1950, in what was to be his last year at Blundell's, he received a letter from his mother in Ceylon, telling him that the family could no longer afford his school fees. 'It was a shock', he was to write in his book *Woolf in Ceylon*: 'I had no idea of our financial troubles.' He had left home as a member of a privileged colonial family with his father, a charismatic figure who 'could lead anybody anywhere' and 'sell anybody anything', presiding over the management of a prosperous tea estate. But in 1948 Ceylon won its independence from the British Empire and this had a disastrous effect on the export of tea. The end of a political era was to produce a family upheaval in which Ondaatje's father sank into debt and alcoholism and his mother had to leave her husband. 'I was obliged to start from scratch', Ondaatje wrote. He found himself at the age of seventeen in a London bank and afterwards emigrated to Canada, not returning to Ceylon (which by then had changed its name to Sri Lanka) for forty years.

For his colonial childhood Ondaatje retains an emotional sense of nostalgia though acknowledging that it is a lost world and that the dismantling of the British Empire was inevitable. The writer who now travels the modern world is a dedicated post-colonial, full of curiosity and a willingness to deal with the unexpected challenges. He is still the outsider who at Blundell's learnt the wiles and strategies of cricket as a method of, and a metaphor for, escaping ill-treatment, overcoming inconvenience and transforming his outsider status into an asset. I do not know which team he supports these days when England plays Sri Lanka at cricket. What I do know is that he transferred his cricketing ingenuity to international finance, making good all that was so shockingly lost in his young adulthood. He has also, as it were, taken over the position of a beneficent colonial power in his role as patron. At Blundell's he had learnt to find happiness though his love of English literature. It is this happiness, illuminating *The Last Colonial,* which he has pursued all his life.

MICHAEL HOLROYD

PROLOGUE:
SEDUCED BY THE
WRITTEN WORD

Though a good deal is too strange to be believed,
nothing is too strange to have happened.

Thomas Hardy, 1871
(from *The Personal Notebooks of Thomas Hardy*,
ed. Richard H. Taylor, 1979)

WHEN I WAS DESPATCHED to England from Ceylon in 1947, over half a century ago, to 'get a decent education' (according to my parents), I was a sallow, thin, frightened thirteen-year-old who was very uncertain of where he was or indeed why he had come. I had been transplanted from a carefree wilderness life on my father's tea plantation in the Kandyan foothills and shoved into Blundell's – a boarding school famous in the West Country of England. My parents had certainly clothed me well, but I had no idea how to behave or speak properly. It was a terrifying foreign world. English schoolboys could be very cruel to strange-looking new boys, who were almost immediately subjected to a raft of traditional rigours and tests such as 'Bim-shaving', in which first-termers were forced to push a collar stud with their nose along the entire length of a floor beam in the large junior dormitory. We were clad only in thin pyjamas, and senior boys whipped our taut bottoms with tooth-brushes dangling from lengths of string. It was a painful experience. If we pushed the collar stud off the beam we had to start again.

We also had to learn, and be tested, about the school. What was the height of the school tower? *Seventy-two feet*. When was Blundell's founded? *1604*. Who was the head of the school? *Robert Nind*. What happened if the River Lowman flooded the school foundation stone? *The school automatically got a half-holiday*. Which Old Blundellian wrote a famous West Country novel? *R. D. Blackmore*, author of *Lorna Doone*.

I learned fast and well, and quickly discovered when to keep my mouth shut and when to make myself noticed. My uncle, the Reverend David Cockle, who had married my father's sister, was my official guardian. However, he was the vicar of Timberscombe in Somerset – too far away to give me the constant advice I needed. My school life was a matter of sink or swim.

Two things saved me. First – cricket. Thank God for cricket. I was crazy about the game, as was everyone in Ceylon, and I had a natural aptitude for it. When the summer term rolled around I was tested in the nets and immediately put into the Junior Colts team. I became a somebody. It didn't matter how I looked or what kind of accent I spoke with.

The second saving grace was English. I began to love English literature as a subject. Even in the junior form, Lower IV B, we had two very good English teachers, Peter Brooke-Smith and S. H. 'Sam' Burton. They introduced me to the novels of Thomas Hardy and R. D. Blackmore, and later to one of Daphne du Maurier's books. I owe my love of literature to them. They taught me everything: the power of the written word, the joy of reading, and eventually how to express myself in writing. It was from them, too, and the books we studied, that I acquired my love of the West Country. I never got the West Country out of my system, even though I emigrated to Canada in 1956. Three decades later, in the mid-1980s, I returned from Canada to the West Country with my wife and bought Glenthorne – an isolated pre-Victorian manor house in the north-east corner of

Devon, perched on a cliff above the swirling Bristol Channel. It is where we live today.

The first Hardy novel we had to study at Blundell's was *The Mayor of Casterbridge*, written in 1886. Here Hardy proved his ability to handle tragedy in a self-assured way, showing his respect for his protagonist, the hay-trusser Michael Henchard who becomes a mayor. I think this is the first novel in which Hardy fully explores tragedy: it pervades *The Mayor of Casterbridge*. Despite Henchard's unhappiness and his wretched death on Egdon Heath, fear somehow seems more associated with the narrator than with the central character. This was a tough beginning for a young student of English born in tropical Ceylon, but it introduced me to Wessex, an absorbing region of fantasy which until the arrival of Hardy was only a historical term defining the south-west of England that had been ruled by the West Saxons in the Middle Ages. Understanding the geography, history and culture of Wessex is of course of prime importance in coming to grips with Hardy's novels.

After *The Mayor of Casterbridge*, I read *Far From the Madding Crowd*, a novel written earlier, in 1874. Its success – which fixed the newly created Wessex in the minds and imaginations of readers – enabled Hardy to give up his job in architecture for writing, and to marry his first wife, Emma Gifford – a marriage soon to produce intolerable strains. For me, the pleasure of *Far From the Madding Crowd* was its vivid portrayal of the artisan community in the villages. The brotherhood shared by workers on the farm is the fertile context for the romances of the young farm-owner Bathsheba Everdene and the unselfish devotion to her of the shepherd Gabriel Oak. It engrained itself in me, to the extent that since then I have compared every English novelist to Thomas Hardy.

The other set book for Blundellians was *Lorna Doone*, published in 1869, a quarter of a century after its author left Blundell's. Blackmore, like Hardy, did different work before becoming a writer.

He was initially called to the Bar, but his occasional epileptic fits, almost certainly caused by beatings and bullying at Blundell's, forced him to take up country life, first as a schoolmaster, then as a fruit grower. He was a reserved and eccentric man with an amazing gift for dramatic story-telling. Happily married, but with no children, he produced several volumes of poetry and thirteen other novels, but his fame rests entirely on *Lorna Doone*. All of his novels lovingly describe the climate, wildlife and vegetation of the West Country, and to some extent its history. I suppose I owe something of my present life to Blackmore. Glenthorne, which he mentions in *Lorna Doone*, lies below and next to Yenworthy, the Ridd farm, and 'up-over' from Oare Church, where the wicked Carver Doone shoots Lorna on her wedding day.

The third West Country novel that I encountered was *The King's General*, the first novel Daphne du Maurier wrote while living at Menabilly, the reclusive Cornish house outside Fowey where she lived and worked for seventeen years. She loved the place and used it for the setting of Manderley in *Rebecca*. *The King's General*, set during the time of the English Civil War (1642–46), describes the effect of the war on Devon and Cornwall. It fascinated my teenaged mind, with its story of a beautiful heroine, deformed by a tragic accident, who falls in love with Richard Grenville, the proud but insensitive king's general. The novel is spellbinding, steeped in romance and history. I think there is a hint of du Maurier in every West Country novel.

At Glenthorne we are surrounded by historical and literary drama, by the classic works of Hardy, Blackmore, du Maurier and other West Country writers. Michael Holroyd and Margaret Drabble live just seven miles down the coast from Glenthorne at Porlock Weir; and Victoria Glendinning is not so far away, in Gilcombe near Stourhead in Somerset. My brother Michael wrote a great part of his novel *The English Patient* one summer at Glenthorne. And most of my own work, including these stories, has been done in Glenthorne's haunted first-floor study looking down the North Devon coast in the early hours of the morning. There could not possibly be a better place in the world to write.

MIKE WHITE'S
IMPERIAL JAZZ BAND

Man, if you gotta ask you'll never know.

Louis Armstrong, when asked what jazz is

'MIKE!' I SAID with amazement. 'Is that you?'

Some time in the mid-1970s, about five years after starting a successful brokerage company with a couple of others, I hailed a Diamond taxi cab in Toronto's Bay Street and jumped in the back. I asked the driver to take me to a nearby insurance firm, so I could deliver a research report we had done on a company. The driver acknowledged my instruction, but said nothing more, and I didn't catch his voice. But while we were coursing our way north on Yonge Street, the back view of his head suddenly seemed familiar. It had to be Mike White.

'How are you, Chris?'

'My God, Mike, I haven't seen you for ages. It must be over fifteen years. How are *you*? And what have you been up to since then?'

'Well,' he said slowly, 'it's quite a long story. But you look good. I read about you in the *Globe and Mail* once in a while – so I guess you've landed on your feet. I knew you would. We talked about it often enough, didn't we? I think you were wise to get out of Toronto and go to Montreal, though all of us in the jazz band thought you were mad back then.'

'Listen,' I said, 'I have to stop in at the Crown Life for just a minute to deliver this report. Promise to wait for me and you can drive me back to Bay Street. Please wait, and maybe we can have a coffee or something.'

'Don't worry', said Mike. 'I'll be here.'

Jazz was the common bond between Mike White and me – first in England, then in Canada. In the early 1950s jazz was still fresh and exciting in London, and tickets to hear the best players were cheap enough for us to afford. I remember going several times together to the London Jazz Club at 100 Oxford Street to hear Humphrey Lyttleton and his band. Mike was then a budding trumpet player and said he wanted to chuck his job as a greeting-card salesman and start his own band. He left London a while before I did. In Toronto, his musical dream soon came true – maybe too soon.

As a teenager, I became fascinated by the traditional jazz that originated in New Orleans in the early 1900s. Very different from modern jazz, trad New Orleans jazz had melodic cornet leads backed by harmonic trombone, a melodic clarinet and a strong rhythm section. One of my favourites was the simple blues-inflected style of the one-eyed Joe 'King' Oliver. King Oliver was the most influential cornet player of his time, the founder of one of the earliest New Orleans jazz bands, and the mentor of Louis Armstrong. In the fifties, I used to collect records by Oliver and Armstrong – 78-rpm discs on the Gennett, Columbia and Okeh labels. I wish I still had them; they are worth a small fortune.

I knew that Joe Oliver had been born on a plantation in Louisiana. He lost one of his eyes in a childhood accident. His mother worked as a cook for several white families but she died early, leaving his elder sister to look after him. Eventually he found work as a butler to a family in New Orleans – a job he kept for nine years. First he played in marching bands; later on in Storyville, the city's red-light district. Aged twenty-one, he became leader of his own Olympia Band and also played with the trombonist Kid Ory, who had his own band. It was Ory who nicknamed Oliver 'King'. Around this time Oliver gave the young Louis Armstrong one of his old cornets, and sometimes they played together. 'Jazz and I grew up side by side when we were poor', said Armstrong. 'I sure had a ball growing up in New Orleans as a kid. We were poor and everything like that, but music was all around you. Music kept you rolling.'

When the bars and brothels in Storyville were closed down, Oliver moved to Chicago, where he formed King Oliver's Creole Jazz Band. Eager to add a second cornet, he sent for his young protégé, who had taken his place in New Orleans with Kid Ory's band. The new band was a sensation. It was Oliver who gave Armstrong the nickname that would stick to him – 'Satchmo' (satchel mouth). The two cornet players were so close 'they wove around each other like suspicious women talking about the same man', said another Chicago band-leader, Eddie Condon. The other members of the band included Lil Hardin (the future Mrs Armstrong) on piano, Johnny Dodds on clarinet, Honore Dutrey on trombone, Bill Johnson on banjo and Baby Dodds on drums. The band recorded classics like 'Dippermouth Blues', 'Snap It' and 'Chimes Blues'.

Yet it didn't last. Armstrong surpassed his master and left to play in New York. He and Oliver were briefly reunited in 1926 but by then Oliver, stricken with gum disease, had started to lose his teeth, as well as his money when a Chicago bank failed. He ended his days in abject poverty, unable to play his cornet, working as a janitor in a pool hall. King Oliver was only fifty-two years old when he died in 1938 and was buried in an unmarked grave in New York.

Anyway, to get back to Mike White, after he went to Canada, he founded his Imperial Jazz Band. They were a bunch of enthusiastic traditional jazz musicians, including a brilliantly creative clarinet player from Scotland, Ian Arnott, who played in a fashion very similar to Johnny Dodds. They began to perform regularly on Wednesday nights at the Maison d'Or nightclub in Toronto.

Encouraged by what I heard of Mike's success, and discouraged by my job at a London bank, I got on a boat for Canada in April 1956, with only thirteen dollars in my pocket, to begin a new life.

Mike had rented an apartment for me in Leaside, a suburb of Toronto, for ten dollars a week including breakfast. It was my first base in Canada and I will never forget my first impression of it, soon after arriving from Union Station.

The apartment was in the basement of a small red-brick house, 19 Parklea Drive. This must have been built in the 1930s towards the end of the Depression and was badly in need of painting but otherwise neither more nor less exhausted than its neighbours. Access was by a separate entrance at the side of the house. My landlady, Mrs Eaton, unlocked the door and showed me down the stairs to my room. A dank pungency clung to the air as I reached the bottom of the steps and saw the wet bedsheets my hostess had hung in the warm corridor that led to the boiler room. Layer upon layer of steadily dripping sheets chilled my sinuses. I felt as if I had entered a super-efficient humidifier. The 'apartment' Mike White had arranged for me was just an imperfectly partitioned corner of the basement room. The oil furnace was right beside the single-walled partition, against which was an army cot – my bed. The doorless entrance opened directly into the tiny corridor. The so-called apartment was basically a laundry room.

But it was somewhere to live. A diminutive chest of drawers huddled in one corner, so I methodically transferred my things from a battered suitcase to the chest, carefully stood my guitar in an unoccupied corner, lay down on the cot and closed my eyes. About four hours later, I woke from perhaps the deepest sleep I had ever had. It was 11.30 on Saturday night and I was ravenous. Somehow, I located a Fran's Restaurant in the new Leaside shopping centre up the road. I took my time going through the menu. The cheapest item was something called 'Chilli and Toast', priced eighty-five cents. 'Is it hot?' I asked the waiter. 'Not too hot', he replied. 'OK, I'll have that.' The beans and gluey mince were an unexpected bonus. My first meal in Toronto. Then I went back to the laundry room, and back to sleep.

I badly needed a job. So I joined the 'cage' – the accounting department – of Burns Brothers and Company, a stockbroking firm. Essentially, the work meant keeping books of clients' equity and bond positions. I worked hard even though I hated it; at least it was a foot on the ladder of finance. What made life interesting was my relationship with Mike, which began to grow into a very good friendship as soon as we got together again.

We met at the Northgate Tavern after I finished work and before he went to the Maison d'Or for his first jazz session at 8 p.m. I hadn't seen him for a year or two since he left London, and immediately I noticed a change. He was still confident and cheerful, but his pale-blue eyes, which had always seemed focused on some remote object visible only to himself, now seemed even paler and almost vacant, with his gaze turned totally inwards. His high forehead topped by a shock of sand-coloured hair, his sparse eyebrows and eyelashes, and his sallow cheeks lent a spectral quality to his features that had not been there in London. He was thinner, too. It was difficult not to suspect substance abuse.

I looked at his trumpet case and said, with an effort: 'I see you're ready for the evening.'

'Yeah. Sorry I'm late . . . got talking to my agent about a recording date, and . . . you know . . .'

'Good God!' I said: 'Don't worry about that. You used to do strictly one-night stands, now it's records. That's fantastic.'

'Yeah, really.' Mike was almost drawling. 'This group of mine . . . Everybody's talking about the great jazz revival here. Steady work at the club, agents bugging me . . . Yeah, it's great. We're really on the scene.'

His speech had a trance-like quality in keeping with his gaze. I felt almost compelled to interrupt, to keep the pace and energy of the conversation at a level appropriate to a reunion of old friends. If I allowed Mike to continue with his monologue, I had the impression his voice would grind to a halt like an old 78 record on a wind-up gramophone in need of a crank.

An aproned waiter was hovering. Mike threw a pile of change on the tabletop. 'Two draughts, please.' The amber glasses came down off the waiter's tray and two dimes from Mike's pile of change disappeared into the apron. We lifted the beers and Mike looked absently into his glass for a moment. Then he smiled at me. 'Well, cheers . . . as we used to say.'

'Cheers, Mike.' I took a sip while he finished all but one finger of his beer at a single hoist. When he surfaced, he leaned forward and asked with a half-smile: 'So what made you finally decide to come over to the colony? The good life? Lure of adventure? That idea of yours you could make a killing if you could just get the breaks?' Mike seemed a little more animated, now that he had a beer inside him. He appeared almost to focus on my face.

'A combination of all three, I guess. Actually, you were one of the people who influenced my decision. Things didn't improve in the bank and I could see myself moving sideways for the next ten years. I figured if I was going to bust out then I'd better do it now. And here I am.'

Part-way through my explanation Mike signalled the waiter for another round of beer. He was not fully listening. What I had taken for signs of animation were merely the stirrings of someone in need of some sort of stimulation. The situation was a bit uncomfortable. I swallowed the rest of the glass, and two more full ones were promptly put on the table. This round was on me.

As Mike went on drinking, his flow of words increased. He kept up his questioning and soon elicited most of the meagre details of my life since arrival in Canada. Finally he smiled again and said: 'So, you got a job on the Street, and you're settled in that basement place. That's great. You'll be one of the Bay Street boys in no time. Before you know it, you'll be sitting in the red seats at the Gardens for the Saturday-night hockey games with the rest of the crowd.' Mike raised and drained his glass, set it down, and at last became genuinely animated.

'This band of mine is a real breakthrough for this town. A couple of the guys I was jamming with got pretty good while I was in England. One even learned to read music. Then this guy, Ian Arnott, turned up from Scotland and he's an extraordinary clarinet player who plays all the old hot five and hot seven stuff. You'll meet them tonight. We've got a banjo player who's learning fast, and a drummer we can rely on. That's it, except for a new guy on trombone who might or might not fit in. With me on cornet there's just five of us. Somehow we got booked into the Maison d'Or every Wednesday, packing 'em in like flies, and people started taking notice. We work every weekend and we're cutting some tapes next month with this guy I told you about who's going to peddle them in New York. And life's great. We still play all the old stuff... Bunk Johnson, King Oliver... We'll do "Muskrat Ramble" tonight and "One Sweet Letter" – you'll think you're in Oxford Street again.'

'Where do you practice?' I asked.

'Oh, up at this guy Joe Taylor's house. You'll meet him tonight too. In fact he's having a party after the club closes. He has parties all the time... You're welcome to tag along if you like.'

We had a sandwich, gulped down another draught of beer, made our way through the crowded bar into the hotel parking lot where Mike had left his car, and drove to the club. It was not much of a place to look at from the outside: an old brick building about one block down a side street that crossed the main thoroughfare. The original obscure entrance had clearly been tarted up. There were white Tuscan-style columns flanking the door and an imitation gas-lamp on the wall; above, a triangular pediment proclaimed the name of the club, Maison d'Or, in a kind of chancery script plus extra flourishes added with a touch of slapdash.

As we climbed the half-step to the porch Mike said he had to change and get ready for the first set. Why didn't I go right down and find a table somewhere? He pointed me to the top of a narrow stairwell and then disappeared through another door. I descended towards a buzz of talk past faded portraits of the heroes of New Orleans jazz on one wall. I recognized most of them and wondered idly whether the club's patrons knew who Kid Ory or Jellyroll Morton was. I guessed not.

From the doorway of the basement, the exact dimensions of the club were hidden in smoke and darkness. Candles were burning here and there, their flames glinting in the glass tumblers on the tables and flickering as the waiters moved past. By the far wall, I could make out a small podium lit by a coloured spotlight. At this moment it was vacant.

My eyes adjusted and I saw an empty chair at a corner table remote from the stage, and started to make my way over. The couple in the other two chairs shifted a little to make room, but said nothing and carefully avoided looking up. I had already begun to get used to the Toronto chill, the downcast-eyes treatment, and made no attempt to start a conversation. When I first noticed it the week after my arrival, I put it down to my slight swarthiness and an illiberal cast of mind. But my twice-daily streetcar experiences to and from the office gradually persuaded me that the same studied indifference applied without regard to colour, race or creed. Here, I thought, was a city in which all ethnic and racial groups had an equal opportunity to be ignored.

A waitress approached and I ordered a beer, this time at the outrageous price of a dollar fifty.

Just before nine, Mike White's band took their places on the podium, and after the usual tuning up and fiddling with the microphone, Mike introduced everyone. They opened with Lil Hardin's 'Perdido Street Blues', first played by Louis Armstrong in 1926. As the music cascaded from the instruments, an exhilaration I could almost touch flooded the clubroom. My God, I thought, *they really are good! Damn good!* My earlier disappointment with Mike was forgotten, and the notes and the beat carried my mind to another place. Closing my eyes, I let my own improvisation soar and longed to be involved in making music.

Mike and his group jockeyed the number through the solos, the stretch of 'fours' where the instruments and the drums take alternate four-bar stints, and then the wailing, screaming, final chorus driving to its climax with the brass players pointing their blaring horns up at forty-five degrees, as if playing for Gabriel himself.

The pause after the last note was electric, then applause crashed across the room. Joining in, I had a sudden recollection of a music historian in London who had cornered me at a Chelsea party to discuss jazz. After listening uncomfortably to the man's long-winded dissertation on the simplicity of the progressions, the psychological effect of holding a single high clarinet or trumpet note through a chord change, and the way a sliding trombone note emphasized the lead-in to a main chorus, I had looked at him and said: 'Never mind all that – it *swings* because it *swings*!' This was how I felt at the Maison d'Or that night. Jazz's exhilarating effect was something I could never describe, because ordinary language lacked the words. Maybe this is why jazz musicians use such strange terms to describe their art.

Mike's group moved quickly into the next number of the set, a slow blues. My admiration for the trombonist jumped several more notches as he rattled off some of the slide notes at just the right places. More applause. Then came the final number of the first set, an up-tempo rendition of 'Tiger Rag', again highlighting the trombone.

At the end, Mike shaded his eyes from the spotlight and peered around the room. Suddenly he was making his way through the tables towards me. The couple at my table straightened up and looked at me with somewhat amazed expressions as Mike said loudly: 'Hey man, come on over to our table. You can buy me a beer.'

I got up and followed him through the crowded room, pleased to have the spotlight of attention focused my way. Mike's group was seated at one of the larger tables near the podium. I shook hands with Archie Walker, the trombonist, and mumbled a compliment, then was introduced to Joe Taylor, a smallish dark man in his early thirties. Three girls, all English, were presented next and I tried to look inscrutable but interesting as I said hello to each of them. It must have been clear that I came with the master's seal of approval because I was immediately included in their talk.

For the rest of the evening I stayed at the head table. The crowd grew from near-capacity to standing-room-only during the last set. The latecomers seemed more boisterous and less appreciative of the music than the early nucleus of jazz buffs. It was obvious as the band swung into the last numbers that they were hot and tired, but this mood was all the better for the playing of improvisational jazz.

When it was over, Joe Taylor invited me to his house for the party, the official invitation I had been waiting for. I quickly accepted.

I was worried about the bill. But Joe Taylor conjured a twenty-dollar bill from somewhere and pressed the whole thing on the waitress with a magnanimous 'That's all right, keep it.'

But how was I going to get to his house? This was easily solved too. Mike simply asked his friend Joe whether he had room for one more in his car.

Through Mike, I got to know Jerry Laughlin, one of four young singers calling themselves 'The Grads', who were quite popular in those days. They sang the old standards. And through the Grads, amazingly, I got to meet Sarah Vaughan.

The Divine Sarah was booked to sing on a Saturday night at the Colonial Tavern – that great jazz nightclub on Younge Street, below Dundas, in Toronto, which alas is no more. Somehow, the Grads' manager had arranged for them to meet her and had wangled them a stage-front table – as long as they agreed to have dinner. But they had to get to the place early because the house was packed. I went along with them, and so there were six of us at the table: the four Grads, Mike White, and me. We arrived promptly at 6.30 p.m. because we knew the first set would start at 7 p.m. We ordered drinks and dinner from the limited menu. I asked for the special 'Colonial Hamburger', French fries and coleslaw, and I can't remember what the others ordered. But we knew we wouldn't be served our food until the end of the first set – about 8 p.m. And then we settled down for the evening.

Now in 1956 Sarah Vaughan was yet to record my all-time favourite of her songs, the classic Errol Garner–Johnny Burke 'Misty', which she did two years later in Paris. But she had already moved to Mercury Records, in 1954. Of course she had conquered jazz long before she came to Mercury: born in Newark, New Jersey, in 1924, she came up in the same two big bands, those of pianist Earl Hines and vocalist Billy Eckstine, which nurtured her contemporaries Charlie Parker and Dizzy Gillespie. But it was at Mercury Records that she really hit her stride, recording Bob Merrill's 'Make Yourself Comfortable' and the Jimmy Dorsey–Paul Madeira 'I'm Glad There Is You'. These were my favourites in 1956, and that night she sang them both. I listened, utterly thrilled, to her contralto reverberating over the clamour of the club, dripping with honey and pouring over the strings. It is the unbelievable lushness of Sarah Vaughan's voice that seduces you. She can slur a vowel to match her vibrato, and she can radiate warmth through the most subtle love

song, basking in the opulence of her incredible vocal gifts. I was awe-struck.

Promptly at 8 p.m. her first set ended. There was great applause, but no encores. After a few words with her band Sarah Vaughan simply tripped down the steps to our table and said: 'Hi boys and girls. That was fun. It's nice here.' Then, with her ample rear end, she literally bumped me off part of my chair so she could share it with me, and fairly soon ate her way through *all* of my well-done hamburger and French fries, washing them down with a couple of very large gin-and-tonics. She was on great form and stayed with us right through the intermission, chatting about all sorts of personal happenings on the road. Just before the second set at 9 p.m. she asked the Grads if they wanted to do a number with her. Of course they did. They decided on 'Little Boy Blue'. 'What key do you sing it in?' she asked. 'B flat', they said. 'Well, give me a B flat.' So Jerry Laughlin sang a note. 'That's not B flat', she said. '*This* is B flat.' Then they sang their song together.

So we had another mesmerizing hour of Sarah Vaughan's consonants ringing with their unique delicate quaver, as she improvised her way through seemingly impossible phrases. She sang two unforgettable encores including Billy Strayhorn's 'Lush Life', which she had just recorded in New York. When the second set ended, she sat with us for only a little while, then excused herself because she had to fly to Chicago early the next morning for another concert.

What an evening! All my life I have secretly waited for someone to ask me: 'Have you ever met Sarah Vaughan?' Indeed I have: I've had dinner with her. In fact, Sarah Vaughan ate my dinner!

So that's how things went on for many months, indeed for well over a year, after I arrived in Canada. I became part of the jazz set. On Wednesday evenings I would go to the Maison d'Or. It was a wild life, and I seldom got back to my laundry room much before midnight. Weekend parties revolved around Imperial Jazz Band bookings, and in the summer there was the occasional weekend up north in Haliburton where Joe Taylor had a cottage. It was fun. Actually, too much fun. But we were young, healthy, and intent on having a good time, no matter what the cost and inconvenience. Certainly we drank too much, and there were always the girls who tagged along – mostly regulars at the club – so I was never lonely. I learned to pace myself and not get too tired or drink too much during the week because it affected my office work. I knew that the fun couldn't last, for me anyway. I was far too ambitious about finance.

At the very end of 1958, I took the plunge. I resigned from Burns Brothers, left the financial world of Toronto, and moved to Montreal. If it hadn't been for the Imperial Jazz Band, my move would probably never have happened. For I knew that neither the job nor the jazz group was getting me anywhere. I wasn't sad, I simply knew I had to make a break, if I was to get a break. But I also knew that the move spelt the end of my musical fantasy world. Whatever else I might achieve in future, I would never be a member of a jazz group.

In Montreal, life changed dramatically. My first job was to sell advertising for the *Montrealer* magazine, while also writing a column on art. I survived and learned a lot, particularly about publishing. Gradually I came to realize that in Canada to advance yourself you generally have to change jobs. This way, there is an element of mystery about a person's qualifications which, given some lucky breaks and a glib tongue, he can usually polish up to shine most attractively. The *Montrealer* job led to a job with Maclean Hunter, the largest publishing company in Canada, who ran trade magazines and the *Financial Post*. A job on this newspaper meant my going back to Toronto – now with a wife and two young children. Which at long last led me to the investment industry and an offer to work for Pitfield Mackay & Company, a Bay Street brokerage company. This time I was hired not to keep books of other people's transactions and money, but to deal in securities for a newly formed institutional brokerage team. I was in the right place at the right time. We were enormously successful and in fact made more money for the firm than all the other departments and branches put together. This led directly to the founding of our own firm in 1970: Loewen, Ondaatje, McCutcheon & Company, providing research and servicing to large institutions across Canada. We went from strength to strength and were soon making more money than we had ever dreamed possible. This was what I was doing when I hailed that taxi cab on Bay Street a few years later, and bumped into Mike White once more.

It took me only a couple of minutes to deliver my package. Then Mike drove us back to Bay Street. I noticed he had turned off the taxi meter but I said nothing. In less than twenty minutes we were outside my office. I convinced him to park the cab on Temperance Street just north of our office building and have a coffee with me nearby.

In the Honey Dew restaurant I looked closely at Mike and found it hard to believe I was sitting next to my old friend. He had aged considerably, and his hair had started to thin out a little. But he still had his mischievous half-smile. 'Gosh, it's been a long time', I said nervously. 'A hell of a lot of water has passed under the bridge. What happened to the band? Are you still playing? What happened to everyone? Did you ever marry Sylvia?' There were a thousand other questions I longed to ask.

He drank his coffee and smiled into his cup. 'Well, I suppose everything happened. I did marry Sylvia, that was the important thing, but it didn't last. She left me when the band broke up at the beginning of the sixties. There just wasn't any more work. The jazz age was over and nobody wanted to hire a bunch of hard-drinking musicians playing some old-time music. When it was over, it was really over. I haven't seen any of the boys for years but I hear that Ian Arnott – you remember the clarinet player? – is back at his old

35

printing job. Archie went back to Scotland. And Jimmy had always kept his office job anyway; so he didn't lose out. I don't think anyone plays any more. Joe Taylor's still around, working as a sports reporter for the *Telegraph*, but everyone else seems to have gone away . . . back to their old way of life.'

'I had a bad time. Not just with the band, but also with alcohol and drugs. It was hard to kick all that stuff. It was OK when you were playing to full houses and all that, but not when you didn't have anything going, and didn't have any money. Things got really tough, you know. We had it so good, and then – which we never expected – we had it really bad. I went to England for a while, because I could get drugs on prescription there. That helped. But kicking the habit was hard. Luckily I have this girl I'm seeing now who's really good to me. We don't have much. She works, so we get by on what we earn. No more stars in the skies and no more stars in our eyes.'

He looked up from his cup. 'I'm glad Canada has been good to you, Chris. You took a hell of a gamble coming here and it really worked. You put your head down, and you set your sights on what you wanted and where you wanted to go. I guess I could have made it with the band. We really had talent. And we worked hard at all the arrangements – just like the old guys in New Orleans and Chicago. But in the long run it didn't work out for them either. Funnily enough, most of them wound up driving cabs too, when there wasn't any music. The strange thing about show business is that it doesn't matter how good you are or how much talent you have, if the public don't want you, they don't want you. You can't change that. When we had it good, here in Toronto, all the jazz greats, most of them now forgotten, used to come up here to play with us. Turk Murphy, Buck Clayton, even Teddy Wilson. Remember him? He used to play piano behind Billie Holiday. I guess we were the only game in town, in fact one of the few games in the whole of North America. It was a phenomenon. It lasted for a while, and then it fizzled out. It wasn't our fault. It's just that we had nothing to fall back on. No insurance. Nothing to do when the music stopped. Nowhere to sit; nowhere to go.'

'Hey Mike,' I said, 'I want you to do me a favour. Firstly, how much do I owe you for the taxi?' 'No way', he replied. 'Nothing. It's on me. Glad to do it, and really glad to see you.' 'OK. But I want you to take this.' I slid two fifty-dollar notes, folded, across the table into Mike's hand.

He flattened them out, one on top of the other, and kept looking at them as he kept ironing out the kinks in the paper, all the while looking down with that half-smile of his. 'You always were a generous person anyway, even when you didn't have any money. You never welshed on a round of drinks and always brought a bottle or a six-pack to our parties. But this is really nice of you. Thank you. I guess my old lady will like me for this. It's a bit of a bonanza.' He kept flattening the notes on the table, rubbing the edges with the tips of his fingers. And then, when he had done just about as much flattening as he could, he put a salt shaker on the notes and gazed at me, still smiling.

'It's great to see you again, Chris. We did have some good times, didn't we? It's great that we were able to play the old tunes when we were young enough to do it. It was a very special time. But now I must get my old cab out of hock and start to work. You guys on Bay Street will be wanting to go to lunch or something, and if I'm not there I'll miss the business.'

And with that, keeping his left hand on the notes, Mike stood up, reached out with his right and shook my hand, smiled, and thanked me once again for being so kind. Then, abruptly, he turned, walked out of the restaurant without looking back, and vanished in the lunchtime crowd. I looked down. The two fifty-dollar notes were still on the table.

I never saw Mike White again.

A CHRISTMAS CRISIS

Frank, if you want to do a movie about me committing suicide, with an angel with no wings named Clarence, I'm your boy.

James Stewart to Frank Capra,
director of *It's a Wonderful Life*, 1946

HAVE YOU EVER stayed alone at Christmas? I mean, absolutely alone? Well I have – and the experience changed my life, although not in quite the way I had intended.

It was the Christmas of 1958 and the winter was extremely cold. Deep drifts of snow lay on the roads of Montreal, the ice on the pavements was treacherous, and a bitter east wind was blowing across the city. I had just moved there from Toronto after chucking up my stockbroking job in the accounts 'cage' at Burns Brothers. The job had been leading me nowhere for a couple of years. I knew I had somehow got to break away and start afresh – maybe in publishing. So I had given up $55 a week, collected together what little money I had (and it was very little), and grabbed the night train from Toronto's Union Station.

My sole introduction in Montreal was to a young man, Stuart Horne, who ran a boarding house on Côte des Neiges. This was called Amherst House and at one time it had been lived in by General Amherst, who commanded General Wolfe's troops in Quebec in 1759. I've always liked history, but my immediate problem in the here and now was how to rustle up $150 in advance for the monthly rent at Amherst House. I simply didn't have the money. So I pawned my typewriter for $200 and made my way to Côte des Neiges, where Stuart Horne gave me a single bed in the downstairs library. I felt really lucky to have anywhere at all to stay and silently praised myself for having got a good deal on my typewriter. There were only two people staying there, because every other resident had gone away to family or friends for the Christmas holidays. I remember the date of my arrival clearly: Monday, 22 December 1958. I had no job, knew no one, and had barely enough money to survive for a month.

Three days later, on Christmas Day, I was the only person in residence at Amherst House. The place was quiet – almost as quiet as a grave – and of course it was cold. General Amherst's huge library windows, with their tattered curtains, hardly kept out the freezing winter draughts. But eventually I plucked up courage to peel myself out of the narrow bed, shave, put on as many clothes as I physically could, then think about what I was going to do for my Christmas breakfast.

Funnily enough, although my situation was miserable, I felt excited. For the first time ever I was totally alone. I knew then that whatever I would do in my life I would have to do for myself.

There was no food in the house. I decided, just so as to fill in the time, to walk all the way down Côte des Neiges to St Catherine's Street and treat myself at one of the cafés to a big meal of bacon and eggs. I set out around ten o'clock. The walk down icy Côtes des Neiges was a long one. Although I had wrapped myself up as far as possible, my overcoat, muffler and woollen hat – pulled right over my ears – did not keep out the bitter wind, while the ice and snow soon soaked my thin leather shoes, making the journey even more uncomfortable. Many of the cafés and restaurants were closed, but eventually, after an hour's walk, I found a tiny café on St Catherine's Street. By this point I was far too cold to be hungry: more important than food was some warmth, away from the street. I decided to stay in the café for as long as they would allow me. Toast, two pats of butter, fried eggs, crisp bacon and a mug of piping hot coffee, then a second mug, filled my stomach. Life now wasn't exactly wonderful, but neither was it all that bad.

After breakfast, I would have liked to have gone to church, but I had no idea where to go. Moreover, my clothes made me a little ashamed. So I trudged aimlessly further down St Catherine's Street, braving the winter weather, looking at all the closed shops, including the windows of a department store. Practically no one else was walking, and there were very few cars on the slippery Montreal streets either. I had no idea what to do for the rest of the day.

Past noon, I found myself in front of a tiny movie hall, the Bijou Cinema. But that too was closed and would not open until two o'clock. Still, here was an idea. If I went to the cinema, I could spend the afternoon in comparative warmth. In the meantime I had about two hours to kill, so I continued to walk east, as far as St Lawrence Boulevard and then back again. Luckily the cinema opened half an hour early and there were a few other people buying tickets. The film was a fairly old one, *It's a Wonderful Life*, which I had heard of but never seen.

Seeing this film by sheer luck turned out to be the best Christmas present I could ever have imagined.

It's a Wonderful Life, based loosely on a short story, 'The Greatest Gift' by Philip Van Doren Stern, was produced and directed by Frank Capra. It is a terrific film, now regarded as a classic, which the American Film Institute rates among the best one hundred American films and number one on its list of the most inspirational American films of all time. But when it was made in 1946, it failed to win a single Oscar and was considered a commercial failure.

The film's setting is the fictional American small town of Bedford Falls after the Second World War. It stars James Stewart as George Bailey, a man whose imminent suicide on Christmas Eve attracts the attention of his guardian angel, Clarence Odbody, who is sent to help him in his hour of need. Much of the film is told through flashbacks spanning George's life, narrated by two unseen senior angels who are training Clarence for his earthly mission to save George and thereby earn his angel's wings. In these flashbacks we see all the people whose lives have been touched by George and the difference he has made to the small-town community in which he has always lived.

When George was twelve years old, he rescued his younger brother from drowning after he fell through the ice on a pond. Later, as an errand boy in a pharmacy, he saved his boss from mistakenly filling a child's prescription with poison. Later still, having married his childhood sweetheart Mary, on their way out of town for their honeymoon they witness a run on a bank that leaves the town's Building and Loan Society in danger of collapse. George and Mary give the $2,000 they have saved for their honeymoon to the towns-people. But things go from bad to worse. George misplaces $5,000 he has to deposit in the Building and Loan Society. When he appeals for a loan from a powerful slum landlord, Henry Potter, to save the society, the Scrooge-like Potter refuses. In panic, George crashes his car into a tree during a snowstorm and runs to a nearby bridge to end his life. He is worth more dead than alive, he feels, because of his $15,000 life insurance policy. But George's guardian angel intervenes and shows him a nightmare vision of what the town of Bedford Falls would have been like, had George and his good deeds never existed – a horrifying slum called Pottersville, with a main street dominated by pawn shops and sleazy bars. In the nightmare vision, his younger brother was drowned; his boss was convicted of manslaughter; and Mary, his wife, is a spinster librarian with failing eyesight and a broken heart because she didn't marry George.

In the end, George begs his guardian angel to let him live. His prayers are answered and he returns to Bedford Falls with a new outlook. He finds that his friends have raised a huge amount of money to rescue both him and the Building and Loan Society. At a party his brother proposes a toast to George as 'the richest man in town', not only because of the many individuals he has helped but also because of the enormous difference he has made to the town. George Bailey realizes that, despite some awful problems, his life really is wonderful.

When I walked out of the Bijou Cinema in the late afternoon gloom of Christmas Day 1958, I felt as if I were walking on air. Despite the snow and the sleet and the wind, I no longer felt cold and my own problems seemed surmountable. I was alone but I knew that my family, though thousands of miles away in Ceylon and England, were all well and, I hoped, having a marvellous Christmas together. It made me feel better just to think of them. I had made the right decision to break away and seek a new life in a new country. A new world lay at my feet. There was opportunity around every corner, and everything was up to me. Life felt great.

It's a Wonderful Life remains a favourite film. Over the years since 1958 I have urged every member of my family to watch it – particularly at Christmas. I see it every year, and each time the film reminds me of my lonely first Christmas in Montreal. I can't help wondering how things would have turned out for me if I hadn't stumbled on it at this particular moment in my life. I also wonder how many lives of other people it has changed, even though, like me, they didn't believe in angels.

OLYMPIC VICTORY

The day when a sportsman stops thinking above
all else of the happiness in his own effort and the
intoxication of the power and physical balance he
derives from it, the day when he lets consideration
of vanity or interest take over, on this day his
ideal will die.

Baron Pierre de Coubertin,
founder of the modern Olympic Games

IN THE WINTER OF 1964, the announcement that a Canadian bobsled team would compete in the ninth Olympic Winter Games at Innsbruck roused no more interest than a tiddly-winks tournament. To the general public in Canada, bobsledding meant almost nothing. Canadians knew about tobogganing, skating and skiing, but not bobsledding. It is a highly specialized sport that consists of driving a two-man or four-man sled, built to rigid specifications, down a twisting ice chute approximately a mile long, at speeds approaching ninety miles an hour. It can be practised only on a run specially built at enormous expense, and in 1964 there were only about twelve of these courses in the world, mainly in Europe, in the Alps, with the exception of one in North America, at Lake Placid in New York State built for the 1932 Winter Olympics. Not a single course was in Canada. If you are driving a sled, bobsledding feels something like racing a car downhill – a car without any brakes, gears or accelerator, controlled only by the precise movements of your hands on the steering ropes or wheel. It is a thrilling spectator sport despite the fact that a person perched beside the run sees each sled for just seconds as it hurtles by. But few Canadians had had the opportunity to watch a bobsled competition, and very few indeed had taken part in one. Naturally enough, it was the skaters, skiers and hockey players heading for the Olympics who caught the public imagination.

So there was not much support for the eight-man Canadian bobsled team, all of them amateurs, except for an official subsidy from the Canadian Olympic Association covering only their travel expenses. They were 'somewhat regarded as underdogs', the president of the association admitted later. When the bobsled team were quartered in Innsbruck, an official of the Canadian Olympic Ski Team said scornfully: 'They're just taking up beds in the Olympic Village!' Although the *Toronto Star* sports editor cautiously rated the team as a 'possible bronze' in the two-man competition, another Toronto reporter got a cheap laugh with a column that depicted the team as a handful of Montreal playboys who embarked on the venture after getting together one night 'over a flagon of sarsaparilla'. Sarcastically he added: 'All Canadians will be overcome to learn that none of these lads has been on a sled since last February. We don't want to take advantage of anybody!' He did not explain that any Canadian who wanted to practise bobsledding would need the time and money to visit a bobsled run in Europe or the United States, and to make special arrangements to use the run while he was there.

To everyone's astonishment, the almost unknown Canadian team won the gold medal for four-man bobsledding at Innsbruck, beating the favourites, the rival Austrian and Italian teams. It was the only gold medal won by Canada at the 1964 Winter Olympics.

I was one of the eight team members – probably the first man from Ceylon ever to compete in international winter sports. For me the whole experience, which began as a bit of a lark in 1960 but rapidly became more and more serious, was a marvellous fantasy that came true. No one gave us a hope in hell of winning. I was incredibly lucky to be part of it. Pride surged through my veins when the Canadian team walked into the arena for the Olympic opening ceremonies. I knew then, probably for the first time, what it meant to be a Canadian. One is always conscious of being an immigrant. After the 1964 Olympics there was little doubt that I was indeed a Canadian. I could stand tall. This is the story behind our team's entirely unexpected victory.

Although Canada took forty years to field an Olympic team, bobsledding is a particularly appropriate sport for Canadians. The earliest toboggans, purely functional sleds consisting simply of a number of poles lashed together with thongs or roots, were built by the North American Indians. In fact the word 'toboggan' is Canadian, deriving from a word in an Algonquian language. Tobogganing as a sport probably first began on the slopes of Mount Royal in Montreal and below Montmorency Falls near Quebec City about 1880. Over the years, bobsledding gradually evolved from a haphazard slide down an open slope in a wooden toboggan, still a popular pastime of Canadian children, to a precise descent of an iced chute in a metal sled designed as carefully as a racing car.

Two Americans on holiday have been given credit for introducing tobogganing into the Swiss Alps, where it developed into three separate sports: Cresta riding, luging and bobsledding. The Cresta or skeleton is a bare sled, without steering equipment or mechanical brakes, on which one man lies prone, with head and legs extending beyond the frame, and steers by twisting the runners with his wrists or digging in the spikes on the toes of his boots. In luging, one or two riders sit upright on a sled with two runners; it was first included in the Olympic Winter Games in 1964 for both men and women. Bobsledding, the most sophisticated of the sled sports, is supposed to have been born at St Moritz early in the 1890s when an ingenious sportsman named Wilson Smith lashed together two sleds with runners and covered them with a plank. The name came from the fact that in the early days the crew sat aboard the sled leaning as far back as possible, then at a signal 'bobbed' upright to start the sled. As toboggans with runners provided more speed and thrills, many new enthusiasts were recruited and by 1895 the Toboggan Club had been formed. Heavier sleds were built and for the first time weights were added as ballast in an attempt to keep the sleds, then called bobsleighs, on course.

After 1904, a new artificial run made of blocks of ice and wet snow was constructed each year at St Moritz. Many winter sports centres followed the lead of St Moritz and built bobsled runs engineered for speed and comparative safety. In the first Olympic Winter Games held in 1924, in and around Chamonix, a four-man Swiss bobsled team won the first official international championship race. At the outbreak of the Second World War, there were more than sixty bobsled courses scattered on the mountainsides of countries including Austria, Czechoslovakia, France, Germany, Hungary, Italy and Switzerland. But after the war, this number fell dramatically. Increased speeds demanded that runs be very carefully constructed so that they retained the same features each year, with nearly perfect ice surfaces, while the addition of safety features added to the cost of construction and maintenance.

Canadians first became involved in international bobsledding early in 1954 when Lamont 'Monty' Gordon, an undergraduate in business administration at the University of Western Ontario, read an article about Douglas Connor, a Canadian who had just broken the world's toboggan record on the famous Cresta run at St Moritz. The idea of hurtling down the serpentine curves of the mile-long ice chute filled Gordon with such excitement that he promptly resolved to head for St Moritz as soon as he finished university. He infected a sportsman friend on the same university course and in the same fraternity, Victor Emery, with the same fever. Together they became the driving force that propelled Canadian bobsledding to the Olympics ten years later – Emery as the driver of the winning four-man bobsled, Gordon as the driver of the second Canadian sled.

After graduating from university in the spring of 1955, Emery and Gordon worked their passages across the Atlantic as deckhands and contrived to spend many months in Europe, ending up in St Moritz at the New Year. They were eager to experience Cresta riding and bobsledding in the company of some of the international sportsmen who used to gather in St Moritz, great natural athletes like the young Spanish nobleman, the Marquis de Portago, who had the money and temperament for pastimes with an edge of danger. Soon the two Canadian friends were hopelessly addicted to bobsledding.

The sensation is probably closest to parachuting in those moments before your chute opens, especially if someone else is driving the sled. You feel your face being squashed into peculiar shapes by the immense blast of cold air. You are very conscious of the bulk of the man sitting in front of you, and of your own hands clutching the narrow metal handholds at your sides. Your body, with every muscle tense, is suddenly assaulted by enormous forces of acceleration and gravity. When you slam over bumps on the corners of the run, each blow comes thudding up your backbone and through your skull. The brake-man at the back of the sled takes the most punishment when the sled whips if it touches a corner. You do not hear the noise of the watching crowd because your ears are filled with the extraordinary chattering roar of tempered steel on ice, so loud that the driver has to bellow out commands, which are used only in emergencies. If he is in desperate trouble, he may be forced to shout 'Brake!' If his goggles are coated by a shower of ice, or are steamed up, he yells 'Goggles!' to the man behind who slips them off downwards so that they do not fall on the track, since anything dropped on the track disqualifies the team. But there is no time to be frightened, because the run is all over very quickly, within just over a minute.

Emery and Gordon had to leave St Moritz two days after the 1956 Boblet Derby – where they finished eighth out of twelve teams – but they were both determined to find time and money to continue their bobsledding careers. Their temperaments were very different: Emery was the more single-minded, Gordon more of a gambler and faster than Emery when his luck was in. But both of them responded to the challenge of bobsledding with such contagious enthusiasm that, in spite of a discouraging lack of official support, over the next few years they managed to continue practising in Europe and to catch and hold the interest of a group of friends who formed the nucleus of a Canadian team.

In 1960, the two of them had a lucky break. It was announced that the 1961 world championship in bobsledding would be held at Lake Placid across the Canada/U.S. border. Without this decision, the Canadians would probably never have fielded a full Olympic bobsled team in 1964 at all. In 1960 they had only two practised drivers and no equipment of their own. They were terribly short of money. If the championships had been scheduled for St Moritz, Cortina or one of the other European runs, it is doubtful if Canada could have sent even four bobsledders. Without years of experience in international competition, they would certainly have had little chance of success in the Olympics. But because it was possible to go to the 1961 championships by car, instead of having to raise thousands of dollars for air fares, Emery and Gordon were able to persuade a dozen of their friends in Montreal, including me, to try bobsledding. They promised, at the very least, a thrilling winter holiday within easy reach of Montreal. In fact, they hoped that some of their friends would be infected by their own obsession with the sport, and join them in a serious bid for an Olympic medal in 1964. They knew that all of us were frustrated athletes, in our twenties, looking for a last chance to accomplish something really worthwhile.

At a key meeting in the spring of 1960, we formed the Canadian Bobsledding Club. First, we decided that everyone present would race, and that we would send a full Canadian team to every world championship right through to the Olympics. Second, we decided to launch an immense drive to raise money by selling associate memberships. This would serve two purposes: it would provide the club with much-needed funds, and would create public interest in a virtually unknown sport. Third, we decided that all the money we raised would be used to buy two four-man sleds, one new and one second-hand.

The active club members (now numbering twenty) contributed money, which was sent as a deposit to Dandria Podar of Italy. Podar, the engineering genius who had built the fastest bobsleds in the world, eventually delivered four sleds to us in Canada, all manufactured in his small workshop in Cortina, which cost a total of $5,400.

Because of the terrific punishment a sled must take, it looks at first glance like a crude piece of equipment, all steel pipe and angle-iron. In fact, the moving parts are carefully made by hand and have extremely close tolerances. The Podar sled had lost none of the strength of its robust predecessors, and was very much faster. You can recognize Podar's achievement as prodigious when you realize that he was able to accomplish, in his basement workshop, something that General Motors Research and Development Corporation was not able to do in its first two attempts to build a faster bobsled. Mainly by trial and error, Podar learned how to design a sled that gave each runner maximum freedom to rotate about its axle, but a minimum tolerance to move in relation to its pair. He devised a number of damping devices to smooth out the rough ride, and completely redesigned the steering mechanism to give a very positive steer with little backlash. By applying a great deal of ingenuity he was also able to provide for conversion from rope steering (preferred by Emery) to a steering wheel (preferred by Gordon) with the least possible effort.

Having learned to drive in Europe, Emery had trained on sleds equipped with ropes in the European fashion. Rope steering is done by attaching a piece of rope about four feet long to each end of the steering bar at the front end of the sled. The driver holds the ropes by means of oval steel rings attached to their free ends. As he sits in the driver's seat, with his legs almost straight out in front of him, the rings should be near his knees. He steers to the right by pulling the right rope and simultaneously easing tension on the left rope with his left hand. It takes some practice to learn how to keep both taut. Any slackness would let the sled run free, out of control. When a sled is running at ninety miles an hour, in a vertical position thirty feet up an iced wall, and it hits a rut unexpectedly, the driver and his team have only a fraction of a second to make the correct movements. The sled can be steered from full right to full left with about a six-inch movement of the steel rings.

If ropes are so difficult to manipulate, why are they used at all? They are so much more sensitive than a wheel that drivers who prefer ropes claim they can feel the sled moving over the ice better, and react more quickly to correct a skid. In the straight, the sled can be allowed to run free and find the path of least resistance down the tracks left by the last sled. If the driver were a fraction off, he might be ploughing snow and losing valuable time.

A steering wheel, which is much easier and more natural to use, was preferred by most American drivers. Since the Lake Placid course had longer and wider straights than most European runs, they claimed that a wheel helped them to keep the sled on a straight path, especially in the notorious Zig-Zag curves when the sled was running fastest. The great advantage of a wheel is that the sled can always be held firmly. Its main disadvantage is its lack of sensitivity and its inherent backlash.

Monty Gordon, who had driven a sled with a wheel at St Moritz in 1959, preferred the wheel but at first tried to use ropes. He never really overcame his tendency to over-correct on the straights. He had several hair-raising crashes at Lake Placid traversing Zig-Zag and coming out of Shady Corner and as a result his brake-man, Gordon Currie, was bruised enough to spend some very restless nights. As the number two man on four-man sleds driven by Gordon, directly behind him, I was generally luckier than Currie.

Sharing the run with teams from fourteen other countries, including Austria, Belgium, Germany, Great Britain, Italy, Spain, Sweden, Switzerland and the United States, we Canadians had an opportunity to observe the different outlooks and attitudes of each nationality. The Belgians were popular and eager to visit Montreal and its famed night-life. Several were titled and only one had ever bobsledded before. As sledders they were hopeless but charming. The Spanish were wildly reckless drivers concerned only with enjoying themselves to the utmost limit of their physical ability. The likeable but inscrutable Swedish team and the humourless Swiss team spent much of their time running up and down in track suits, seemingly as concerned with the physical shape of their bodies as with the condition of their sleds. The Italians were friendly and helpful, but obviously prepared to win. Everyone regarded them as the favourites and they had their teams and equipment under perfect control all of the time. The Italian sleds were in immaculate shape. Having sanded and polished the runners to smoothness, the Italians insisted that they must never touch ground until the race started, and actually kept the sleds in their hotel rooms at night. We were impressed and discouraged; we felt no one else could have a chance against the superb coordination of the Italian team.

Despite very good performances by Emery and Gordon, the Canadian sleds were badly beaten in the two-man races. Eugenio Monti of Italy won his fifth straight world championship in two-man bobsledding, and a young U.S. Marine from Lake Placid finished a surprising second. Another Italian got the bronze medal. Emery drove the Canada II sled to finish ninth, and Gordon finished twelfth with Canada I, ahead of the Austrians, the Spanish and the Belgians. Sadly the four-man event had to be cancelled because of warm weather and hazardous track conditions. Returning to Montreal, we had lots to talk about, but we had lots to do, too, and lots of money to raise before we could get a team over to Germany for the 1962 championships.

In December 1961, the Canadian Amateur Bob-Sledding and Tobogganing Association officially announced the nine-man team that would represent Canada in the championships at Garmisch-Partenkirchen. It also announced, at long last, that it was now officially affiliated with the Amateur Athletic Union of Canada. This was an important step. Without such affiliation our team would not have been able to get the recognition we needed to represent Canada at the Olympics in 1964.

Vic Emery had to drop out, temporarily, because of urgent university examinations in his course at Harvard, but his brother John Emery, another of the original enthusiasts for bobsledding in 1956, was able to get away from his medical training in Britain to take Vic's place. In Gordon and John Emery we had the necessary two drivers. As at Lake Placid, I was part of the team.

Garmisch-Partenkirchen is a resort in the extreme south of Bavaria, almost on the border with Austria. It lies in a junction of two deep Alpine valleys at the foot of the Zugspitze, the highest mountain in Germany. Garmisch is one of the most beautiful villages in the world, and the towering Alps on either side dwarf the houses and the people. Famous as a ski centre, it was the scene of the 1936

Olympic Winter Games. Garmisch and Partenkirchen were originally two separate villages, which were united just before the Olympics.

The training runs started promptly on arrival at the crack of dawn and we were immediately astonished by the improvement in Gordon's driving. Relaxed and confident as he had never been before, he was clearly one of the top four or five drivers present, and in for a great season. All through the trials, both he and John Emery drove well and very steadily. The Garmisch run was a difficult one and we were amazed how quickly our two drivers mastered the tricky turns and straights, apart from one spectacular crash by Gordon in the Kasparseck curve, which was terrifying at the time but in a strange way quite exhilarating, and fortunately left me with no serious injuries. John Emery, who had driven only a few times in his life, showed great natural ability, and Peter Kirby, his brake-man, gave him some very useful help. However, the championship runs were a little disappointing for our team. The Canada II sled, driven by Gordon, came in fourth, and the Canada I sled, driven by John Emery, finished twelfth out of fourteen teams. Even so, the Canadian team was awarded a cup for the most improved bobsled team. Back home in Canada, we got letters of congratulation from senior members of the Amateur Athletic Union, which gave us a good feeling. The Calgary Olympic Development Association – formed to promote Banff as the site of a future Winter Olympics – invited Vic Emery to offer advice on the layout of what was projected to be Canada's first bobsled course. (It was eventually built in 1988 for the Calgary Olympic Winter Games.) But we knew that there was now only one more practice year before the 1964 Olympics at Innsbruck.

It was to be a rough year for the Canadian team. The 1963 championships were held at Igls, a little village near Innsbruck, on the same run scheduled for the Olympics. Vic Emery, after a year's break for his studies at Harvard, was back in the team. This time I was not selected. So I was not there for a bad crash by Gordon during a training run. Due to warm weather, what had been a small bump ahead of corner twelve had developed into a jump, and the light and skittish two-man sleds were becoming airborne. On his second run down, Gordon came off this jump crooked and as a result had to pull his sled hard over to get it to take corner twelve at all. By the time he was at corner thirteen, moments later, the sled was on an even keel again but on the wrong side of the run. Gordon was not able to get it over to the corner in time and the sled turned over in the soft snow beyond. Brake-man Currie had his head tucked well down and as a result his helmet took the battering against the ice wall, but Gordon had his head thrown back, and his throat was cut open under his chin on the top of the ice walls. Currie was only stunned and bruised and was able to walk, but Gordon was taken unconscious to the hospital in Innsbruck, where he spent several days recovering. He still has the gruesome scar.

This was a bitter blow for the team, but fortunately nobody was permanently injured. The run was closed for major repairs. Vic Emery had had only one ride down the course, since he had been in the line waiting to follow Gordon. His time had been the third fastest to date and he appeared to be in wonderful mental form to give the Italians a run for their money, but Gordon's crash undoubtedly upset him. John Emery was hurriedly recalled from the luge run and Gordon's steering replaced with the ropes that John preferred. He had the unenviable task of starting cold in the championships with only three days' practice on inferior equipment. On the day itself, the Italians came out top again. The two Canadian sleds finished eighth and twelfth in the two-man event, and ninth and twelfth in the four-man event – creditable, but no improvement on their performance in the previous championships.

Gordon's serious accident at Igls was a sobering reminder that bobsledding is a dangerous sport. But he got back into shape during

1963, determined to compete there again in the Olympics. The rest of the team's Igls experience had been useful in several ways. They had a chance to take the measure of the challenging and treacherous course. Vic Emery had been able to renew his skills after a season's absence. John Emery got some very valuable driving practice, so that the team could for the first time pick from three drivers instead of two. All the other team members also strengthened their experience – an advantage because almost all the 1963 team members returned to compete in the Olympics. In addition, I rejoined the team, and Doug Connor was appointed coach. Connor, whose Cresta riding at St Moritz in the 1950s had inspired Vic Emery and Gordon, had become five-times world champion Cresta racer. His keen competitive spirit was to be enormously helpful to the bobsled team. Stan Hamer, an inventive contractor and marina operator, and a former mechanic with the Royal Canadian Air Force during the Second World War, was a real boon to the team in looking after the equipment and managing chores. Charles 'Chuck' Rathgeb was appointed manager. For the first time, we felt we were competing on equal terms with the European and United States teams.

In early January 1964 we were ready to go. Since the Igls run was closed for practice until the week before the championships, we went first to Cortina. Here Vic Emery proved that he was the most consistent of the three drivers and Gordon was conspicuously inconsistent. On most days Vic Emery, Gordon and John Emery placed in that order but Gordon usually had the fastest and slowest times of the three. At the end of the week, and primarily because of one spectacularly fast run, Gordon averaged a fractionally better time than Vic Emery, and John seemed to be dropping further back in the field.

The Cortina run seemed to have a lot of sand in it, which scored our runners and caused many hours of work trying to eliminate the scratches with emery cloth. Little did we know at the time that this was to have a decided psychological advantage for us before the

Olympics were over. In frustration, Peter Kirby coined the phrase 'speed grooves' for these scratches. When we began to put in the fastest times in the early heats of the Olympics at Innsbruck other teams began to feel wary of our 'speed grooves', and we too began to talk of them with long and serious faces.

Ever since Lake Placid, when the leading Italian bobsledder Eugenio Monti had repeatedly emphasized the supreme importance of a good start, we had been watching other teams' starts and trying to perfect our own. In order to get the greatest possible momentum at the top of the run, a team must be superbly coordinated. In the starting zone that extends just fifteen metres (some fifty feet) behind the start line, the members of a four-man team form up with their hands on the push bars of the sled, rock it in unison, and push like hell. Our particular rhythm was always 'one . . . , two . . . , three . . . , push, push, push', with the driver, then the number two man (my position), then the number three man and finally the brake-man jumping aboard at the precise instant he felt he was no longer likely to reduce the speed of the sled. If a man's timing is just slightly off, he will add part of a second to a sled's time. If a man pushes the sled a fraction too hard, he could cause a crash even before the sled starts. If someone stumbles, the sled will almost certainly have lost the race.

The two-man bobsled championship was run on 1 February 1964. Canada II, driven by Vic Emery, came in fourth; Canada I, driven by John Emery, was eleventh. Vic still had an excellent chance of winning a medal; John was already out of the running.

But now the weather turned warm and wet, with no fresh snow. Four-man training was inevitably delayed. Unable to practise, we instead watched our hockey team as they sneaked by West Germany four goals to two, and edged the United States team eight to six. The hockey players were the glamour boys of the Canadian team. We were impressed and encouraged when they came to watch one of our four-man championship runs.

In the end, we got only one day, 4 February, of official four-man training. The run was in amazingly good shape considering the warm and wet weather. Vic Emery, driving Canada I, was calm and relaxed and drove right down the line on both his runs, one of which was the fastest of the day. Gordon, driving Canada II, was still having trouble with the top half of the run. After all our practice on the starts, we were a little disappointed by our starting times – but half of the team had done nothing for ten days.

Emery's four-man team was now attracting a great deal of attention from the public and from other competitors. Our supporters began to talk about the possibility of placing in the top three. The pressure on the whole team started to mount. Without warning, we were all told that each of the heats constituting the championships would be advanced by a day because the weather was so uncertain. The meet officials wanted to be sure that they would have a chance for all four runs, and by advancing the heats they gave themselves a day's leeway.

Before we went back to the Olympic Village that night we went over our sleds again with a fine-tooth comb, polished the 'speed grooves' on the runner blades, and weighed in our sleds with the judges. Nothing remained now but to get out there and do our best the following morning.

That night there were only about two degrees of frost. But it was enough to keep the run in fairly good shape.

The following day, 5 February, was a great day for Canada. Vic Emery, with two runs of 1:02:99 (equalling the existing track record) and 1:03:82, was in first place. The two Italian teams – one of them captained by Monti – were lying in second and third place, respectively. Monty Gordon was in eleventh position with two runs of 1:04:63 and 1:04:43, his best times to date. With a lead of almost a full second over Monti, Emery was in a commanding position.

Then the organizing committee changed its mind again. With two runs completed, the committee decided to split the remaining two runs, allocating the third run to 6 February and the fourth to 7 February, thus prolonging the tension and pressure (and increasing the gate receipts).

On 6 February, there was a little snow in the air but it did not amount to anything. After one bad moment when he mislaid his lucky beaver hat – subsequently found in plenty of time – Emery drove a perfect course. Unfortunately his running position was very near the end and by the time his team pushed off, the course was slowing down and getting very rutted near the bottom. As a result Canada I ended up with only the second fastest time of the day but increased its lead on everyone except for Austria I, who vaulted into second place. Canada I's time was 1:03:64. Canada II, my team, had a very rough ride, but improved its placing to tenth with a 1:05:06 run.

We again occupied ourselves for three or four hours putting the sleds in order, and then spent a quiet evening at the hotel. On the surface we looked calm and relaxed but underneath we were like volcanoes ready to erupt. The tension was electrifying, but there were no last-minute crises. Vic Emery tried to avoid conversation, yet still appear confident and unconcerned. On 7 February, both of the Canadian sleds were among the first to be transported up to the top of the run, and by the time the whole of our team had arrived, the sleds were upside down on their trestles with one man rubbing each of the eight runner blades.

The night before, the organizing committee had decided that each team would be given a pilot run, to make up for the lack of training time. Canada I zoomed down in the second fastest time. By now the British team almost to a man were working with us – carrying the sleds, polishing the runners and protecting Emery and his crew from the press, television and well-wishers. The British were too far back in the running to stand a chance of winning, ditto the United States team. The British therefore urged us to win for the Commonwealth, while the Americans urged us to win for North America.

At last the championship runs began, each team pushing off with a roar of encouragement from the crowd. Both Canadian sleds were in the second half of starters, with Canada I running third from the end, following by Austria I and Monti's Italian team. As the times were announced we realized that the run was gradually slowing, but as long as there were no serious delays, this would have no effect on the final rankings. The weather was still overcast and cold, but the track was becoming rough and rutted again.

Soon it was Canada II's turn. A last hand-shake all round with no comments made, followed by 'One . . . , two . . . , three . . . , push, push, push' – and we were gone. It was an average run, neither better nor worse than our other runs.

Next came the second Italian team. They managed a fast time, the fastest of the day by 0.05 seconds, and a reminder to the three teams to follow that one mistake could cost them first place.

Canada I was next. Willing hands moved the four-man sled into position, and a hush descended on the crowd. Dead silence. 'Bob frei', the starter droned. The gate was lifted, and they were free to go when they wanted. The team stepped into position and snapped the sled back and forth a few times. The big 'zug' was alive and ready to go. Beaver hat under his seat, goggles down, Emery was ready too. 'One . . . , two . . . , three . . . , push, push, push', and with a roar from the crowd they too were gone. Emery's time for the first fifty metres (164 feet) was announced – very good; time half-way down – very fast; three quarters? – lost some time but still fast. Emery had ticked coming into the feared Hexenkessel corner and had a tense moment getting lined up again. He ticked coming out, once, twice, and then was back in the groove and finished with the second fastest time of the day. He was off his sled in a moment and, grim-faced, was pacing up and down. Two more sleds were still to come, and both could beat him – especially Monti, the Italian veteran who could work miracles with a bobsled.

Austria I cracked off the best starting time of the day, as they had consistently throughout the competition, and drove a strong race. But they got only to within one tenth of a second of Emery's time on the fourth run.

Then it was Monti's turn. By the time he was half-way down the run, we knew he could not do it and that Canada had won. We waited in a tight little group until the Italian sled swished up to the finish. Its time was announced and Emery stepped up to slap Monti on the back and then – pandemonium! The Canada I team – Vic Emery, Doug Anakin, John Emery and Peter Kirby – were hoisted onto the shoulders of the British team members and linked arms in one great self-congratulatory hug. Cheers rang out, flashbulbs flared, and the frantic television camera crews tried vainly to get a good shot of the celebrations.

Emery's final aggregate time over four runs was 4:14:46, more than a second faster than the Austrian sled at 4:15:48 and Monti's Italian sled at 4:15:60. The Canada II sled, driven by Monty Gordon, with me as number two, David Hobart as number three and Gordon Currie as the brake-man, had a total aggregate time of 4:19:78, and came in fourteenth.

The sleds were quickly stowed away, and we all went to the Sport Hotel in Igls for a victory celebration. All but two of the other teams turned up to offer us their congratulations and to sing a traditional song. The party ended just in time for the official prize-giving ceremony and the Olympic award in the hockey arena. The champagne we had drunk made the trip to the podium in the centre of the ice more hazardous than the bobsled run at its worst. By eleven o'clock that evening our nervous energy had completely dissipated and Canada's big day at the 1964 Winter Olympics was over. Late that night it started to snow. The fall, which kept up intermittently for five days, came too late for the competitors but perhaps it was symbolic for the residents of Innsbruck. They must have been glad to see an end to all the Olympic sound and fury and to start life anew with a clean layer of snow.

'SUICIDE' BIRDS

*I am driven on by the flesh; and he must
needs go that the devil drives.*

William Shakespeare,
All's Well That Ends Well, Act I, scene iii

THE BIRDS PLUMMET out of the sky without warning in their
thousands, perhaps hundreds of thousands (no one knows the true
number), they hover, and then they crash into the hillside. They
come every autumn, at the end of the monsoon months, always on a
moonless and foggy evening, between 6 p.m. and 9.30 p.m. And only
to Jatinga, a tiny village on a ridge in the North Cachar Hills district
of southern Assam. Almost fifty species are involved, including
doves, pigeons, bitterns, herons, kingfishers and eagles, some of
which are rare and exotic: the red-headed trogon, the spangled
drongo, the blue-breasted quail, the khalij pheasant, the paradise fly-
catcher, the maroon oriole, the veenal hanging parrot, the scimitar
babbler, the silver-eared mesia and the blue-winged minia. To begin
with, the local Jaintia tribal people of Jatinga assumed that spirits had
descended from the sky to terrorize them. Then they began to kill the
birds for food, using long bamboo poles to bring them down as they
hovered and torches to disorient them further. But still the birds
returned – year after year after year. No one has yet been able to
explain what drives them to commit 'suicide' at Jatinga. Presumably
winds at high altitude, fog and lack of moonlight all contribute
to their abnormal behaviour, but despite research by naturalists this
unique and extraordinary phenomenon remains a mystery.

The person who first mentioned the 'suicide' birds to me was a friend from my Canadian publishing career, the Norwegian mountaineer Arne Naess. We were booked together on a flight to England from Bermuda in 1985. The hills and mountains of India were then much on Arne's mind, because he had just returned from leading a highly successful Norwegian assault on Mount Everest, which strangely included the English mountaineer Chris Bonnington among its seventeen members, all of whom made it to the summit and back.

Although Arne was in a very weak state, having lost a lot of weight, we talked through the night, his voice sometimes dropping to a faint high-pitched whisper. 'You know, Christopher, they say you have to give one hundred per cent in order to climb Everest. But they are wrong. You have to give a hundred and twenty per cent nearly all the time. And death is always around you: frozen bodies, discarded oxygen tanks, graves. Oblivion is only inches away. And endless exhaustion. You are forever fighting the elements and yourself. There are others there, but this is a lonely business. You know that if you do not have the will to survive – it is a simple matter to choose death over life.'

Arne Naess, born Arne Raab in 1937, was the son of a German ski-jumping coach and Kikki Naess, from one of Norway's most prominent families. His uncle, Arne Naess Sr, after whom he was named, was a famous mountaineer, ecologist and philosopher who in 1950 led the first ascent of Tirich Mir in Pakistan. When his parents' marriage broke up after the Second World War, Arne moved to Norway with his mother, and changed his name from Raab to Naess. Although his German birth meant that he was picked on at school because of the wartime Nazi occupation of Norway, he eventually won the admiration of his peers with his daredevil exploits. His uncle introduced him to climbing in his teens. Rumour has it that Arne celebrated his last day at school in 1956 by climbing the National

Theatre in Oslo and leaving his school cap on the building's spire. Eventually he left Norway to work in New York for another uncle, Erling Naess, who taught him the shipping business. By the late 1960s, when he became a director of my Canadian publishing company, he was estimated to be worth $100 million, and by the time of his death he was said to be a billionaire.

Something about the Jatinga birds clearly fascinated Arne. As a climber, he had had several close encounters with death. At one point in our long night-time conversation, he asked me point blank whether I had ever contemplated suicide. I said I hadn't, although I had written about it in a novel, *Fool's Gold*, the story of a young financial adventurer who loses everything on the stock market. He seemed fascinated. In reply he said he too had never considered suicide, but, like the Jatinga birds, he forever felt the urge to flirt with death. It was like a magnet for him. He had never thought the Everest expedition would succeed, he said. Or if he were to get to the summit, he had thought he would never be able to return to base camp.

We remained friends, even after I sold all my North American business interests in 1988 and returned to England to concentrate on exploration and writing. By then, Arne had left his first wife to marry the American singer Diana Ross, whom he had met in the Bahamas. He once brought her along to my publishing company's annual meeting, causing quite a stir among the shareholders. Their turbulent marriage ended in 1999.

I met Arne Naess for the last time in London in 2003 at a screening of the Royal Geographical Society's fiftieth anniversary movie about the first ascent of Mount Everest in 1953. As usual, we talked about the good old times together, the turmoil in the financial markets, and his climbing and my writing ambitions. He told me he had met and fallen in love with a Norwegian girl, Camilla Astrup, but had no intention of giving up his mountaineering career. 'There are still more peaks to conquer', he laughed. 'Some of them have never been climbed.' He seemed very happy and at ease.

So it was a real shock for me to hear a report on the radio in England in January 2004 that Arne had died in an accident on a hitherto unclimbed ridge in the Groot Drakenstein mountains near the town of Franschoek outside Cape Town. According to the report, he had gone climbing alone, having refused a local guide. There was fog on the ridge, so he had decided to return by abseiling down a cliff, as he told his South African host in a phone call. According to the police, his anchoring equipment came loose from the crags and he fell to his death.

Arne Naess died doing what he most enjoyed in his life: flirting with death. As he once told an interviewer: 'If I hadn't liked risks, I would rather have played tennis or golf.' When I heard the news, I immediately thought of his emotional reaction to the Jatinga birds. Both the birds' urge and Arne's drive struck me as equally mysterious.

THE MAN-EATER OF PUNANAI

Leopards do not become man-eaters for the same
reasons that tigers do. Though I hate to admit it, our
leopards – the most beautiful and the most graceful
of all the animals in our jungles, and who when
cornered or wounded are second to none in courage
– are scavengers to the extent that they will, when
driven by hunger, eat any dead thing they find in
the jungle, just as lions will in the African bush.

Jim Corbett,
The Man-Eating Leopard of Rudraprayag, 1947

AT NOON ON 22 May 1924, Captain R. Shelton Agar received a
telegram from the Government Agent, Eastern Province, Ceylon.
'Reward Rs.100/- offered destruction man-eating leopard Punanai
ten miles from Valachenai ferry', it stated. Captain Agar hardly
needed a hundred rupees. He was a prosperous estate owner and tea
planter in the Hatton district, with long family connections in the
colony. But the offer made him 'quite excited', as he wrote later,
because he had never heard of such a leopard before. He had shot
leopards at a water-hole, he had watched leopards kill, he had stumbled upon leopards in the jungle, he had killed rogue elephants and
other mad beasts, but the idea of going after a clever cat with a taste
for human flesh struck him as an 'interesting undertaking'.

In 1989 I wrote a book, *The Man-Eater of Punanai*, a factual book,
which had at its heart only half the truth. Perhaps this is not so
unusual; many a non-fiction writer has embellished or exaggerated,

slightly shifted time or place, fleshed out transients into centre-stage characters – all so as to make a narrative more evocative and more exciting for the reader. But in the case of my book, the opposite was true. It was not that my experiences needed spice, a pinch of creative fabrication to season the humdrum reality of my return to the land of my birth in the 1930s, now known as Sri Lanka. Far from it.

The book was to be a story of exploration and discovery, partly into my own family history, but also into the notorious man-eater of Punanai, a leopard that wreaked havoc, destroying many lives in a small village in Ceylon in the 1920s. My plan was to travel through Sri Lanka, returning to familiar haunts that I had not seen since I was a boy, trying to comprehend what had driven my father's alcoholic self-destruction, taking careful, often frightened steps through a land greatly changed since my childhood and now in the grip of a civil war.

Each evening I updated my journal as fully and accurately as possible, doing my best to capture the sights and sounds and smells of the place, knowing that these notes would form the basis of the book, aware of how quickly such memories can fade. My last stop was Punanai itself, in the north-east, which was an extremely dangerous place to visit at the end of the 1980s. Nevertheless, I was determined to see for myself the scene of the leopard's crimes and its ultimate demise.

On my return to England, I spent long hours at my house, Glenthorne, working on the travel journal, interweaving autobiography, family history and research until a manuscript finally emerged. This was to be my first book on Ceylon and probably the most personal book I would ever write: the symbol of the start of a new life free from the constraints and obligations of the North American business world. My visit had been a bittersweet journey into my own past and I had forced myself to address occasionally painful feelings about my childhood. Here on paper was my struggle to understand my father, here too a record of the astonishing events in Punanai, both in 1924 and in 1989. I was excited, and more than a little nervous, about how my editors might receive it. Their response was not quite what I had expected.

With a few tweaks and revisions (and the addition of my photographs) they said it could make a decent book. But there was one big problem: my account of the trip to Punanai. The editors simply refused to believe this. It was too far-fetched for them: even if readers could credit my meeting an old man in Punanai who had actually seen the leopard, they would never believe the old man's claim that he had survived an attack.

The first time I heard about the man-eater was as a child, the day I saw my first leopard, on a visit with my father to the Yala Game Reserve in 1946. My father was at his best that day. He saw my enthusiasm for the animal, whose elusive beauty caught my attention more than any other animal I saw in Yala. Since then I have often wondered what so drew me to leopards then and draws me still. Many of the big cats share the leopard's grace and majesty, but none has its air of both mystery and evil.

My father, however, was less concerned with the exact cause of my excitement than with encouraging it. He answered my many questions as best he could, but he could not supply the facts and figures a twelve-year-old wanted. So in the evening I turned to our trackers and asked them to tell me everything they knew about leopards. 'Do they eat people?' I asked. And this was how I first heard the story of the man-eater of Punanai. It was, incidentally, also one of my first experiences of the Sinhalese talent for storytelling. Despite the story of the man-eater being told in pidgin English – or maybe because of it – it was gripping: the trackers spared no horrifying detail, no gory description, in bringing the story to life.

The bare outline was as follows. Over the course of a year or two in the early 1920s, an exceptionally dangerous and audacious leopard killed and devoured at least twenty human beings in the region of Punanai, holding the tiny village in the grip of terror. Villagers vanished from their mud huts during the night. Coolies vanished as they worked on the railway lines. Bearers walking empty stretches of the road to Batticaloa were ambushed and eaten. Children were snatched in broad daylight. A state of local panic persisted until Captain Agar finally shot the beast in 1924.

The trackers' retelling frightened me out of my wits. Yala, in the south-east of Ceylon, was really wild in 1946. I incorrectly thought that Punanai was not far away from us. The bungalow where we were staying was remote and exposed. There was only the light of the kerosene lamps, and I had a vivid imagination. Not that it took much imagination, as I lay on a cot on the verandah in the hot night, to fear a leopard moving in the dark jungle just beyond the parapet. So strong were those feelings that they have never left me.

That is why the story of the man-eater became the centrepiece of my book. In addition, I felt it had a link with the civil war. The conflict between the Tamil Tigers – officially known as the Liberation Tigers of Tamil Eelam (LTTE) – and the Sinhalese in the north and in the east of Sri Lanka had been going on since the early 1970s, but by 1989 the situation had become significantly more complicated. Conflict between rival Tamil factions sprang up in the Tamil-dominated north, while the anarchist JVP were active in the Sinhalese-dominated south. Meanwhile, both the LTTE and the Sri Lankan government wanted to oust sixty thousand peacekeeping troops sent to the north and east by the Indian government of Rajiv Gandhi. This was the violent confusion into which I walked. I received many warnings about the dangers of doing this or that, going here or there, especially to Punanai. The final goal of my safari lay right in the heartland of Tamil Tiger territory.

Access to Punanai lay through guerrilla-infested jungle. The LTTE had wrested it from the Indian troops and were of course being opposed by the Sri Lankan army. Neither side wanted strangers in the area. My driver, Mahinda Rajapakse ('Raja'), was worried for my safety, but refused to let me go alone. Although Sinhalese, he had dark skin and spoke Tamil fluently. He warned, however, that I could be mistaken for a foreign correspondent and the threat of ambush was real. I must not appear to be too eager for information or photographs.

We drove in silence through arid scrub and tall grass – ideal ambush country for both leopards and human beings. But we saw no one until just to the west of Punanai when two armed soldiers waved us down at an LTTE checkpoint. They took Raja into a hut for questioning. Where were we going? Why? Didn't we realize the danger? Did we have any weapons? Who was the foreigner? Why was he interested in a man-eating leopard from long ago? But after about ten minutes we were allowed through, having promised not to stay too long, not to discuss the political situation with the local people, and not to report on it when we left. The armed LTTE soldiers left us in no doubt that they thought we were crazy.

At last we reached the village of Punanai. At the edge of the road there was a ramshackle stall selling ginger tea. We stopped to talk to some of the villagers and I couldn't help but notice the guns lying in the grass nearby. I drank in silence, nervous and glad to have something to do with my hands, but Raja chatted easily enough with the young men. We asked for a second cup. Then Raja asked if they had ever heard a story of a man-eating leopard or its killer, Captain Agar? We were met with quizzical expressions all around and the discussion quickly turned back to the Tigers. But from the corner of my eye I could see an old man dozing in the shade who looked up, startled, at Raja's words. At first he seemed an incongruous figure among the Tamil occupants of the roadside stall. 'Let's ask him', I persisted.

The old man's story proved to be pure gold for my book. His actual words never made it into print; my editors deemed them too incredible. Nonetheless, his story changed my understanding of events in 1924 from a man-versus-beast adventure into something altogether more chilling. No matter how much my editors might scoff, I could not dismiss the old man so easily. They had not seen the certainty in his eyes or experienced the sharpness of his memory. Perhaps, too, they had not seen as many inexplicable events in their lives as I had.

'I saw Kuveni', said the old man. There was a pause while he registered our blank looks. He narrowed his eyes and looked at me closely, as though weighing me up before shrugging and carrying on. 'Ah. You do not know. What I mean is that I saw the leopard, the man-eater. I was there.'

When Raja softly translated this to me, I could hardly contain my excitement. A hundred questions rushed into my mind, but Raja urged caution. We should let the old man tell his own story at his own pace; there was more to be learned by listening. So I simply nodded. Raja smiled at the old man and gently asked him to tell us more of what he knew.

'I was working on the railway, on the extension between Batticaloa and Trincomalee. All my friends had jobs on the tracks. It was good work at first, hard labour, but satisfying and friendly too. There was a good feeling about the railway, that we were building something useful. In the evenings people would tell old tales from the *Mahavansa*. It was like a competition to see who could spin the best story. My friend, Ananda, he was the champion. You could almost see those great characters flickering on the edges of the fire's shadows when he spoke. He made them so real. He made me want to learn about our myths, our history. And I did, after . . . after the man-eater, as you call her. No one ever brought a story to life like Ananda.'

The old man fell quiet, absorbed in his memories. Then he continued: 'Anyway, the mood on the tracks soon changed. One day a man went missing. Then another. We searched and searched but found nothing. Then a third man vanished. This time we found a body, all the soft insides chewed out. Then the rumours started flying. It was a monster leopard, a beast that could appear from nowhere – a flash of white gold in the grass – and could vanish just as fast. The camp became a different place. Everyone was looking over his shoulder. No jokes, no chatter. Some of my friends started sleeping in the branches of the trees. I am not ashamed to say I was scared... Only a fool pretends he isn't afraid. I went to the doctor, the *vederala*, and talked of what was going on. He gave me this.'

The old man held up a pendant that was hanging round his neck. We could see that it was two leopard claws mounted in silver with filigree decoration – a *divi-niya-pota*. 'I wore it for protection', he said. 'And I always carried this with me.' He pulled a large knife from his waist. 'I did what I could to protect myself, but all around men were panicking, wondering if they would be next. Some were so scared they almost went crazy. Some left altogether – they would rather give up their wages than stay and take the risk of being eaten. And it wasn't just us, the railway workers. Villagers were taken too. By the time Manickam went, we'd lost nineteen people to the leopard.'

'Who's Manickam?' asked one of the young men. We weren't the only audience now. The measured intensity of the old man's voice and the raw mystery of his story had drawn in our companions.

'He was the inspector's servant. Inspector Altendorff was his name. He came to look at the track – check its safety, our progress, check up on us. He sent Manickam to post his letters, but Manickam foolishly took a shortcut. I didn't see the body that day, not until later. We were working to clear the tall grass from the side of the road that morning. Hot work, but vital, because we didn't want the creature to have anywhere to hide. Altendorff came running up in a frenzy. Before he could even get his breath back he had picked four of us – the strongest ones with the biggest knives I think! He led us back, cutting a trail though the undergrowth further into the jungle. You could see the blood on the ground. Every step was leading us closer to the danger. It was crazy. After a while the four of us stopped. We refused to go on. To carry on any further would have been certain death and the inspector must have known it. We were all back at the road soon enough, shaking with relief. And then I think the inspector must have sent a telegram because soon another man came, Captain Agar.'

At the mention of this name, Raja asked the old man to pause, to allow him to give me the gist of the story so far. I mentioned that it was only by coincidence that Shelton Agar saw that telegram, that he just happened to be passing through Batticaloa when the news came in. I said to Raja: 'Can you ask him if he knows that Captain Agar had tried to kill the leopard earlier on?'

The old man suddenly seemed to lose interest and I was worried that I had offended him with my interruption. I motioned for him to continue and swore to myself I would not interrupt again. Thankfully, as the old man reached the heart of the story, he seemed to drift even further into the past. His gaze was fixed somewhere else, not on us, as though he could see the characters of his youth acting out their deadly adventure once more.

'Oh yes', said the old man. 'We had all heard about the great captain's battle to slay the leopard. At first he tried to trap her using a goat as bait, but of course she was much too cunning for that. I wasn't surprised to see him come back – he was keen to have another chance. I knew there was a reward for killing the man-eater, but I don't think it was the money he wanted. A man like that didn't need more money. But he had a need for danger. It seemed to me that he thought about the leopard all the time. He was really determined.

'The captain and the inspector took us into the bush again. I nearly refused to go, but I was young then – I wanted my share of the glory, and I had my talisman. Again we walked close to Manickam's trail of blood. One of my friends cleared our way ahead. Then came the captain, another worker, the captain's driver, then me and the inspector and a fourth worker behind us. Each of us holding our breath. I remember all I could hear was the swish of the path being cleared ahead and the irritating buzz of the flies. Then we saw the body. I have seen the remains of many creatures killed by big animals, and I have seen the bodies of men killed by other men too, but this . . . this was devil's work. The corpse was propped up against a *pallu* tree like a doll, like someone who had stopped to take a rest in the shade, but it was naked, its tattered clothes strewn around and the neck horribly bitten. Most of one of the legs was gone, and the belly, eaten out, was trailing across the ground. I nearly ran. The beast hadn't finished and she couldn't be far. But the captain, he was so excited. He ordered us to build an ambush and wait.

'The waiting was almost the worst part. Standing in silence, parts of the corpse before my eyes, imagining Manickam's last moments, the knowledge of Kuveni's power growing in my mind. The white men couldn't know anything of this, but even they were tense, though they tried not to show it. By the time we heard a low growl close by we were all so jumpy that the captain dropped his cigarette. He ordered us to shoot to kill, but clever Kuveni wouldn't show herself.

'It looked like it was going to rain and the sun was beginning to set. The captain insisted we go back to the village for food and lanterns to prepare to wait through the night. It was my job to tie the body to the tree so that the beast couldn't drag it away. I can still feel the roughness of the rope in my hand, and the stickiness of the blood. I was trying to secure the wrists without having to look too closely when I sensed it. Danger. Kuveni must have been watching us all afternoon, but this was the first time I felt her close. I ran and didn't see exactly what happened next. The inspector fired first, I think, and then the captain. He might even have hit her, but still she . . . vanished.

'We went back to camp and returned when the sky was completely dark. The captain went up to the tree to inspect the bait. But it was gone. The body I had tied so securely was gone. That was the only time I saw fear on the captain's face. By now it must have been obvious even to him that this was a leopard unlike any other. We hurried back to safety for the night.

'I thought they might give up after that, but the next morning the captain was even more determined. I felt sick at the thought of returning to the place. But we went back once more and this time followed the trail of the body to where Kuveni had dragged it. We found a skull with just a few strips of flesh still attached. And then we heard a crunching noise coming from the bush. Everyone started moving at once, most of us away from the sound, the captain striding towards it, his gun at the ready. My friend thought he saw her and shot, but it was only a sambur.

'The captain was looking crazed by now. He wanted us to build another platform about ten feet above the ground, where he could hide. The seat and the platform were ready by mid-morning and we dragged the body – what was left of it – to a small clearing nearby. |It was covered in flies. Then we walked away. Two of us took up posts in the surrounding trees and I stood watch at the bottom of a tree some distance from the bait, leaving the captain on his platform near the ambush. Everything felt the same as the day before: waiting, fear, silence, thirst. Only the sound of mosquitoes for distraction. I wondered what the captain was thinking. Did he also think he saw the leopard each time the light shifted over the leaves beneath him? Was he startled by the sudden noises of the jungle – a bird's shriek, the trees creaking? He must have been sweating now, anticipating an attack at any moment, standing so still, so close to the stinking remains of a man whose fate could so easily be his own. But this captain always seemed more excited than afraid. Perhaps he did not know Kuveni as I did, or perhaps he had his own god to guide him.

'I remember the inspector left his post in the afternoon to fetch tea. That was a reckless thing to do. Who knew where the beast might be hiding? But he was loyal to his fellow white man and the captain must have had a terrible thirst. When he got back the rain started. I sensed something. I should have climbed tree instantly, but I was paralysed with fear. She was there, just thirty feet away. Kuveni. Staring across at me, baring her fangs, swinging her tail. Her eyes were golden. I had time to think how magnificent she was before I panicked. Then I was reaching up, those eyes fixed in my mind, my hands scrabbling on the wet bark trying to haul myself up the tree and out of danger before she could reach me.'

The old man paused for breath and his audience breathed with him, each one of us transfixed by his words and by what might come next. But he said nothing for some moments, simply pulling back the cloth of his sarong to reveal his leg beneath. A series of ragged, pale scars stretched along the outside of his thigh, almost from his hip bone, twisting round to the back of the knee. The skin was white and corrugated, standing out against the soft, wrinkled flesh surrounding it.

'My talisman was not working for me that day. Just as I was reaching for a higher branch and safety I felt her claws pierce my skin, pulling downwards to scrape the bone, tearing away my flesh. It was so quick and such a shock I don't think I realized quite what had happened until I turned and saw my blood, my own blood, on the ground. I screamed. Somehow I managed to pull myself up, before she could lunge again. I did not feel the pain until later. But I heard the shot.

'My scream had alerted the others and somehow the captain had got an angle on the beast. He shot her in the heart through her neck.

They say it was a very fine shot. Perhaps my talisman helped me after all, because I was the only man to survive an encounter with the man-eater. They rushed me back to camp for medical treatment and I recovered quite quickly from the wound. It took longer to stop dreaming about it, to stop seeing those eyes, feeling the points of her claws again and again. Everyone else thought that was that: the man-eater dead, the captain a hero. But perhaps he sensed more than he let on. I heard it said later that the captain called the man-eater "some beautiful white devil." Those were his words, "beautiful white devil." And so she was.'

He finished speaking and there was silence. The youngsters lounging around the tea stall, their own guns only a few feet away, were looking at the old man with new respect. When Raja quietly translated the end of the story for me, I could hardly believe it. Perhaps I should not have been so surprised by my editors' doubts. If I hadn't heard the story myself from the old man and seen his scars, I would not have believed it either. But I knew he was speaking the truth, although I was sure that there was still something he was holding back.

'Ask him who Kuveni is', I begged Raja. The old man seemed reluctant to tell more, but after some conversation with Raja, he eventually spoke again.

'My friend, Ananda, told the story of Kuveni. I cannot tell it like he did and you cannot understand how important it was to us then . . .' There was a long pause. 'Kuveni was the queen of the Yakkas, and a witch too. The Yakkas were famous for being able to transform themselves into other forms, other animals. Kuveni seduced Vijaya, the founder of our race. Their children became the Veddas, the tribe who still live near here.

'After some years, Vijaya banished her and married a beautiful princess instead. Kuveni was furious. She wanted to kill him. Using her powers of witchcraft she became a leopard and prowled into his bedroom. But Vijaya was protected by his guards, so Kuveni stuck out her long tongue, a tongue made of crystal, to curse him with its touch. A soldier cut off the tongue and put it in a golden box. But it was too late. The tongue became a leopard again, and when the box was opened Kuveni fled into the night. The king never recovered from her curse and died without having any children. That is the *divi dos*, the curse of the she-devil.

'When we heard Ananda's story, we knew it was true. The man-eater was not really a leopard. And Captain Agar must have sensed it too. It was the she-devil, the *divi dos*. The captain may have killed the beast, but the curse lives on. Just look around you. It is plain to see. The curse lives on.'

THE GARDENS OF
TAPROBANE

*... it was with tremulous excitement that I first
saw the little island of Taprobane, in Weligama
Bay off the south coast of Sri Lanka ... I felt that it
was aware of me, that it silently beckoned, sending
forth a wordless message that meant: Come. You'll
like it here ... The only person who had actually
lived there was the Comte de Mauny Talvande,
who had built the house and furnished it after
reclaiming the island from its former status as
the local cobra-dump.*

Paul Bowles,
'An Island of My Own', 1985

I WAS ONLY TWELVE when I heard the scream on the island of
Taprobane. Actually, it was more like a repeated gasp than a scream,
which was followed by a long, low hissing noise, somewhat like air
being released through someone's teeth. I was on holiday with my
parents, my two sisters and my three-year-old brother Michael.
I remember it happened about three o'clock in the afternoon after
lunch, when we children had been sent to our rooms for an afternoon nap – quite a normal thing to do in the tropics. It was a very
hot late November afternoon. We had been playing and swimming
for most of the morning on the long, crescent-shaped Weligama
beach a short distance from the tiny island, only about two acres in

area, off the south coast of what was still known as Ceylon. At low tide one could easily walk the few tens of yards to and from the beach. But at high tide the water was chest-high and women and children used to be carried by servants to the small pier that led to the entrance steps of Taprobane.

My parents had rented the island for our holiday in 1946. Much later, I discovered that the owners had bought Taprobane for only Rs.12,000 in an auction in 1942. Its previous owner, Count de Mauny Talvande, had died in debt in 1941. De Mauny himself had bought the island in 1925, built a unique and magnificent house there on the red granite rock covered with palms and jungle scrub, and lived on it almost until he died. Our family was staying in what had recently been his home.

Taprobane really is a magical island, which deserves its name. The count christened it with the ancient name of Ceylon, Taprobane, because its shape looked a little like the pearl shape of Ceylon; he ignored its local name, Galduwa. According to his memoirs, *The Gardens of Taprobane* – a rare book published in 1937 – Galduwa had been used by the locals as a dumping ground for cobras, which could not be killed for religious reasons. Eventually, De Mauny got rid of all the snakes, and in 1927 set about building an octagonal central hall, thirty feet high and twenty feet in width at its widest point, with a dome supported by eight square pillars of Wedgwood blue with gilded capitals. He gave this pavilion a fanciful name, the Hall of the Lotus, and had eight wooden panels inlaid around it, decorated with a design of lotus buds and flowers. To quote his own luscious description of the hall, 'This is hung with curtains of soft *eau de nil* silk, a deep brocaded border of *art nouveau* design at the bottom, black and gold on a cream ground. These curtains are kept open during the day, drawn only at night. All the rooms con-verge in to the hall through eight arches; nothing interferes with the full view of the interior, nor with that of the terraces and gardens, which are seen through the carved mullions of doors and windows. A frieze inspired by the Sigiriya frescoes runs along the white stone walls.'

When Count de Mauny had finished making his miniature paradise, he could look northwards from the centre of the hall to the entrance steps through wrought-iron and brass gates set between towering palms and a vast array of tropical foliage. To the north-east, he had a sweeping view up the palm-fringed Weligama Bay. To the east he could contemplate the Italian-style gardens, where the land sloped down to a well, fed by a spring below sea level. Here, overlooking the gardens, was the count's bedroom. He loved to watch the sunrise. And when he looked southwards from another bedroom window over a small triangular lawn, there was nothing except ocean between him and Antarctica. Every morning, the count liked to lie in bed and listen to his gardener raking the leaves off the gravel path with an *ekel* broom. Everything – the house, the gardens, and the furniture of his own design – was in perfect harmony. After a restless and turbulent life in France and England, De Mauny spent many happy years in his unique island home.

As I mentioned, I heard the scream when I was having a nap. I had been given the room next to the count's old bedroom. There were no doors to the bedrooms – only the thin silk curtains that we pulled open and shut along solid brass curtain rods. I knew that no one was in the room next door because my mother and father, who had been sleeping there, had driven to Galle with a tea planter friend of theirs, H. L. 'Tank' Roche, who was staying with our family. They had left us in the charge of our *ayah* or nanny. My sisters and brother were still asleep.

I got up, pulled back a silk curtain, and looked into the count's old bedroom, but saw only his large empty ebony bed. Then I heard the sound again – the long repeated gasp. Somehow I didn't feel frightened, only curious. I entered the room and looked on either side of the bed for something or someone who could have made the anguished sound. But there was nothing at all to see. So I went back to my own room next door, and drifted off to sleep.

When I woke up, I was still puzzled. I asked my sisters if they had heard anything during their naps, but neither of them had. Perhaps I had dreamt up the whole thing. I decided to say nothing about the scream, and pretty soon the strange experience went out of my twelve-year-old head.

Two days later, we waded across the water to the Weligama Rest House for an early evening dinner of fried prawns and fish curry, a favourite with my father. In those days the main road ran behind the Rest House, not in front of it. At low tide you could therefore run down the front steps of Taprobane, splash across the shallow surf in bare feet, sprint over the wide sandy beach and across a little bit of scrub grass, straight into the Rest House.

The food was marvellous and the Rest House keeper, Mr Jayakody, was very kind to our family. We were just having a second helping of buffalo curd and honey, *kitul panni*, when Mr Jayakody jokingly said to me: 'Did you hear it, Master Christopher?'

'Hear what?' I replied.

'You heard nothing? Nothing at all? Which bedroom are you in?'

I told him which bedroom. And then I remembered the scream two days before. I tried to describe it in front of everyone. My father was quite annoyed with me that I hadn't said anything about it before.

'Ah yes', said Mr Jayakody. 'That's the count. He died two days ago, you know, on the 27 November [in 1941]. Of a heart attack. He was visiting a friend in the north of Ceylon, in Jaffna, on the Chelvarayan Estate in Nawatkuli. They buried him up there in St Mary's Burial Ground, which is a Catholic cemetery. It was a real shame, because he always wanted to be buried on his island. He came here with practically nothing, but he built this fabulous house. It was the only place where he was really happy. None of his family went to his funeral, which was organized by an English solicitor he didn't even know. But he often comes back to Taprobane and usually at this time of the year. The gardener hears the sound of him gasping for breath through his open bedroom windows. It's quite a common occurrence, and no one pays much attention anymore. He was seventy-five years old when he died, a little after three o'clock in the afternoon.'

Night had truly fallen when we made our way back to Taprobane with flares and torches. We children were still in high spirits and enjoyed being carried over the high tide by the servants, who made several trips to and from the beach at Weligama to collect us. But my father and mother were unusually quiet. When we reached the house, they collected their bags and clothes from the count's old bedroom and moved themselves to the spare guest room over the servants' quarters facing the beach. For the rest of our holiday, that room was simply left empty.

MURDER IN CEYLON

*It does not often fall to the lot of a man who
has helped in a murder for pecuniary gain that
he should receive a conditional pardon from
those who act in the name of the Crown.*

Justice Gratiaen,
in his summing up of the Ceylon Supreme Court
trial of the Sathasivam murder case, 1953

ON 25 JUNE 1953, John Reginald Halliday Christie of 10 Rillington
Place, London, was found guilty of strangling seven women, and was
sentenced to death at the Old Bailey. On the very same day, by a
strange fluke, Mahadeva Sathasivam, the former captain of the
Ceylon cricket team and perhaps the world's most talented batsman,
was acquitted of strangling his wife and walked free after twenty
months in remand.

The judge in the Sathasivam trial was my uncle, E. F. N. Gratiaen.
Uncle Noel was my mother's brother. He was first a lawyer, then a
judge, and then from 1956 to 1958 the attorney general of Ceylon.
After that he moved to England, where he continued to practise law
until he died in 1971. I had followed the trial closely from England in
1953, but it was not until I met my uncle again in the 1960s that I got
some real understanding of the very complicated murder case that
had shocked the island in the early 1950s.

I went to school in Ceylon at St Thomas's College, where cricket
was a passion. In the mid-1940s we worshipped Sathasivam above
all other cricketers. Educated at Wesley College, he produced many

brilliant innings for his school, including a magnificent 145 runs against St Thomas's College in 1936. He was a right-handed batsman who could cut, drive and pull with extreme power; his late cut was his most revered stroke. Having captained the Tamil Union Cricket and Athletic Club, he first played for Ceylon in 1945 and scored 111 runs against India. Not long after, he scored 215 at the Madras Cricket Club; in 1948 he captained Ceylon against Australia; and in the 1950s, after leaving Ceylon, he captained the national team of Malaysia. Frank Worrell, the West Indian captain, said that the very first batsman he would pick for a World XI would be 'Sathasivam from Ceylon'. Gary Sobers called Sathasivam 'the greatest batsman ever on earth'.

In 1940 Sathasivam married Anandan Rajendra, and the Tamil couple eventually produced four daughters. Miss Rajendra had two valuable properties, as well as jewelry, as part of her dowry. In 1949 one of Mrs Sathasivam's properties was sold and a house, 'Jayamangalam', was purchased at 7 St Alban's Place in Bambalapitiya, a residential area of Colombo. There the couple were living at the time of the murder. By 1949 the marriage was already in trouble, and the following year Mr Sathasivam became involved with an attractive young woman, Yvonne Stevenson, born to a Dutch mother and a Polish father. For a while the Sathasivams separated, and by 1951 they appeared to be headed for divorce.

I had just left Blundell's School in England when I learned that on 9 October 1951, shortly after 3 p.m., the strangled corpse of Mrs Sathasivam had been found by a Meegoda laundryman at the above address, lying face upwards on the floor of the garage with a wooden mortar placed on her neck. Her two young daughters were playing downstairs in the adjoining house. A next-door neighbour, Mrs Foenander, was called and the Bambalapitiya police informed of the crime. By 3.23 p.m., 7 St Alban's Place was under police guard and an angry crowd had gathered outside the front door. A short while later, Mahadeva Sathasivam, who had stayed at 7 St Alban's Place on the night of 8 October but had left during the morning of 9 October, was arrested at a friend's house in Colombo. A nineteen-year-old servant boy, Hewa Marambage William, who also lived at the house, was found to be missing.

Ten days later, after an extensive search, the servant boy William was found in the village of Kalametiya in the Tangalle district on the south coast of the island. He was taken to the Matara police station for questioning about the murder as well as about certain articles – precious stones from a ring and a *thalikody*, a gold bar worn after marriage – that had been stolen from Mrs Sathasivam's neck and later sold. It was also noted that there were eight injuries on William's face, arm and hand. William was remanded in police custody.

The law of Ceylon determined that a magistrate's inquiry had to be held into the murder of Mrs Sathasivam, before a trial in a higher court. The inquiry began on 2 November 1951 and ended on 16 October 1952, when both Sathasivam and William were committed to the Supreme Court for trial.

Then, surprisingly, over a year after the death of Mrs Sathasivam, a pardon for William was offered on behalf of the Crown by the then attorney general (and later chief justice) of Ceylon, Hema Basnayake, 'on condition that William [make] a full and true disclosure of the whole of the circumstances within his knowledge of the murder and abetment of a murder and relative to every other person concerned, whether as principal or abettor in the commissioning of the said offence'. William agreed. Although he was now no longer on trial for murder, he was remanded in police custody until the end of the court proceedings.

The sensational trial before Justice Gratiaen began in the Supreme Court on 20 March 1953. Sathasivam alone was charged with the murder of his wife under Section 296 of the Ceylon Penal Code.

He entered a plea of 'Not Guilty', and throughout maintained that he was not in the house at the time of the murder. The second accused, William, who had been given a conditional pardon by the attorney general, was the chief witness for the prosecution. He admitted acting as an accomplice to Mr Sathasivam's strangling of his wife, at the request of the former – but he denied that he himself was the murderer.

The prosecution produced circumstantial evidence strongly suggesting that Sathasivam, who was well known for his drinking and philandering, had murdered his wife. The crown accused Sathasivam of: (a) manually strangling her, first lulling her into a sense of false security by having sex with her; (b) stamping on her neck with a shod foot after the strangulation; (c) planning the murder in order to throw suspicion on the servant boy; (d) with cynical regard for Hindu custom, removing the *thalikody* that he had placed around her neck on her wedding day; (e) removing other articles of jewelry from her dead body; (f) giving money and the removed articles of jewelry to the servant William as a reward for assisting with the murder; and lastly (g), daubing the corpse's feet with kitchen dirt in order to strengthen the case against William, whose legitimate activities were confined to the kitchen. A motive for murder was also suggested in that Sathasivam was unemployed (cricketers in Ceylon were all amateurs in 1951), with no income except for a small allowance from his mother, and was faced with the burden of alimony in an expected divorce ruling, which would deny him access to his divorced wife's property or fortune.

But the prosecution case had many weaknesses. For example, the precise time of the murder was a key issue, on which the scientific experts who had examined the body disagreed. Without doubt, Sathasivam had left 7 St Alban's Place by cab at 10.30 a.m., when his wife was alive and healthy, according to the Quickshaws cab driver who had seen the couple standing together at the door of the house.

There was a bitter legal battle between the eminent counsel T. S. Fernando for the Crown and Colvin R. de Silva for the defence. The inspector general of police, various police officers, and medical experts including a professor of forensic medicine, two eminent professors of surgery at the University of Ceylon, and the world-acclaimed forensic scientist Sydney Smith of Edinburgh University, offered varying and conflicting opinions. The general public, however, were almost unanimous in believing Sathasivam guilty of the murder. Then, following a fifty-seven-day trial, Justice Gratiaen gave a long, detailed and excellent scientific analysis of the evidence. It was a landmark in the history of law and forensic medicine in Sri Lanka.

His summing up included the damning statement that 'the stigma which attaches to a self-accomplice, a person who has admitted that, even as an accessory, he has committed an offence punishable by death, is not removed merely because an attorney general, however respected, however illustrious he may be in the law, has conferred on him a conditional pardon'. It is no secret that after questioning the credibility of William and severely criticizing the conduct of the police, Justice Gratiaen correctly directed the jury, which then deliberated for sixty-four minutes before bringing back a unanimous verdict of 'Not Guilty'. Three prosecution witnesses were sentenced to two months' rigorous imprisonment for giving 'palpably false evidence on a matter of vital importance affecting the guilt or otherwise of the accused', and a fourth prosecution witness was discharged with a severe warning. William, having been granted a pardon by the attorney general before the case, also walked free after the trial. He is the only person alive today who was a first-hand witness to what happened at 7 St Alban's Place on that fateful day in October 1951. He lives in the village of Angunabadulla in the Thihagoda area eight miles from Matara. Interviewed in 2003 by Ravindra Fernando, a forensic specialist who wrote a book on the case, William continued to maintain that he was only an accessory to the murder committed by Sathasivam.

I recall that the last time I met my uncle, for a drink at El Vino's bar near his London chambers some time in the late 1960s, we discussed the Sathasivam case again. 'They made a terrible mistake in offering William a conditional pardon', he said. 'It was irreversible. All the evidence pointed to his guilt, but he was not on trial . . . only Satha was. Everyone thought Satha was guilty. If he had been found guilty, the wrong man, and an innocent one, would have been hanged.' With my uncle then was Learie, Lord Constantine, a great Trinidad and West Indian cricketer, and the first black member of the House of Lords. The two men were great friends. 'There is little doubt that Satha was innocent', my uncle concluded. 'He was a scoundrel, but not a murderer.' Lord Constantine added: 'He was also a hell of a cricketer.'

CHANDRASENA'S REVENGE

*Revenge is a kind of wild justice, which the
more man's nature runs to, the more ought
law to weed it out.*

Francis Bacon,
'Of Revenge', 1625

ABOUT TWENTY YEARS AGO, while researching my autobiographical book, *The Man-Eater of Punanai*, I visited my father's
old tea estate, Kuttapitiya, at Pelmadulla in the Ratnapura District,
in the company of my lawyer friend Lakshman 'Lucky' Senatilleke.
We spent most of the day with the resident planter, who was running
Kuttapitiya for the government-owned Sri Lanka Plantations
Corporation. It was an emotional visit. The planter's bungalow is in
a glorious position on the very top of a hill overlooking the
Pelmadulla Valley, so that it is usually above the clouds in the early
morning. I had not been to the place for over forty years, since 1947,
the year I last saw my father, when I was fourteen years old. On the
way back down the terrible Kuttapitiya road through the tea slopes
into the lower division, estate people came out of nowhere to greet
me, shaking my hand and calling me 'Ondaatje Putha'.

Our car had just completed the winding four-mile descent from
the bungalow when, just before Robbers' Bridge, without any
warning Lucky abruptly asked the driver to stop in front of a humble
dwelling. On the opposite side of the road from this house a thin
man with a shock of white hair, clad only in a bright red *amudé*
loincloth, was clearing the clay soil with an *alavangu*, a long pointed

steel rod. He stopped working when he saw us, looked surprised when Lucky got out of the car, then walked hesitantly towards him. I stole a photograph of them through the car window. They seemed to recognize each other, shook hands, and became involved in what appeared to be a serious conversation. From time to time the man pointed to the house across the road and then, after a few more minutes of talk, he turned solemnly away and continued his work.

The chance meeting had obviously upset Lucky. For a long time he said nothing. Then, after we reached the main road and were heading for Ratnapura, Lucky told me this incredible story. Of course I have changed the name of the central character, who is still alive.

About ten years earlier, the man we had seen, Chandrasena, had built himself quite a reputation as a Kandyan dancer. Kandyan dancing originated in the central Kandyan hills of Sri Lanka. According to legend its origins lie in an exorcism ritual known as the Kohomba Kankariya that was supposed to have been performed by shamans from India when they came to the island to cure a king who was suffering from a strange sickness. He was tormented by sleeplessness and fatigue, and kept dreaming of a leopard that vindictively directed its tongue towards him. The leopard was really Kuveni, a sorceress and the first wife of King Vijaya, founder of the Sri Lankan race, who was casting an evil spell on the king. After the shamans had performed their dance the king's illness vanished, and many natives of Kandy adopted the dance, which eventually spread to other parts of the island. Although its popularity waned while the British were in control of Ceylon, the dance to some extent revived after the island's political independence.

Chandrasena was a *Ves* dancer. *Ves* is the most popular and pure Kandyan dance and is performed only by males. The elaborate *Ves* costume, particularly the headgear, is considered sacred and is believed to belong to the deity Kohomba. Only towards the end of the nineteenth century were *Ves* dancers allowed to perform outside the precincts of the Kankariya Temple at Kandy's annual Perahera Festival. Nevertheless, because of caste barriers and other political reasons, the most traditional form of the dance is seldom seen outside the Dalada Perahera.

At first, Chandrasena performed his dances only in Kandy. Then, after he had married a younger and very beautiful Kandyan girl, who was also a dancer, he moved to Ratnapura – this was in the 1970s – where he started a dance school. The school taught both male and female students. Originally only males could train as dancers, but then a few special schools were allowed to train women too. As there was no definite *Ves* costume for women, the female dancers were allowed to adapt the male costumes.

For a while Chandrasena's dance school flourished. His young wife, with constant coaching, became an exceptional dancer and teacher. Many students, particularly children, came to learn not only Kandyan dancing but also the Sabaragamuwa dances local to the Ratnapura area, which worship the much-revered god Saman.

But then, as fate would have it, Chandrasena's wife fell in love with another young dancer whom he had hired to teach the children. Chandrasena noticed the growing friendship but at first thought little of it. Eventually, though, their relationship became strained both at home and during the long evening dance practices. Yet it seemed – at least to his wife – that Chandrasena showed no jealousy: he appeared to have decided to ignore what might be a passing infatuation. Instead he concentrated on the task of running a successful and expanding enterprise. The dance school was getting a lot of attention and press coverage, and imitators were springing up. Chandrasena was invited to Kandy and Colombo to speak about his school. He accepted many of these invitations, which kept him away from Ratnapura, sometimes for many days and nights.

However, no one knew what was going on in his tormented mind. Chandrasena was a quiet and resourceful thinker, who seldom shared his opinions with other people.

And then the day came when he was invited to be a principal dancer in the Dalada Perahera in Kandy. He had been away from the city running his school for several years, so the invitation was a great honour. He accepted and set off from Ratnapura with his *Ves* costume. He was not expected to return for some days, because the Perahera usually runs for a fortnight. But immediately after the first day's dancing in the festival, Chandrasena caught the night bus to Ratnapura and then walked the two miles from the bus stop to his simple single-storey house abutting the hall in which the dancing classes were held. It was some time after midnight when he arrived and his house was dark, as he silently let himself in through the front door. Without hesitating, he made his way to the bedroom and found his wife in a passionate embrace with her lover. Again without hesitation, he raised a long *kinissa* dagger and with a single movement plunged the blade into the back of the unsuspecting lover, killing him instantly.

Then he released his hold on the weapon and, ignoring his wife's screams, turned and walked out of the house into the night. Early the next morning he caught a bus to Kandy, where he went straight to the Dalada Maligawa to dance at the Perahera. It was only after the day's dancing was over that the Kandyan police arrested him and charged him with murder. He was kept in Kandy's police station that night, then taken the next morning by van to Ratnapura jail. The murder trial took place three months later. The junior counsel attached to the defence attorney for Chandrasena was Lucky Senatilleke.

Now in Sri Lanka, following British law, leniency may be shown to the perpetrator of a crime of passion when there is proof of grave and sudden provocation. Thus a sympathetic judge can direct and possibly influence a jury to find a killer guilty of manslaughter rather than murder, if the violent act was not premeditated. In this case, it was prompted when an unfaithful spouse was discovered *in flagrante*. Such was Chandrasena's defence. Although, as Lucky explained, it had been a difficult task to prove lack of premeditation, in the end Chandrasena was found guilty of manslaughter, not murder, and sentenced to three years in Gombara prison in Kandy.

After the trial his wife went back to her parents in Kandy. Chandrasena, when he had served his term, went to live with his brother and family in Pelmadulla, where we had just seen him. As he remarked to Lucky, he had entirely given up dancing.

A TEA PLANTER'S STORY

Love and scandal are the best sweeteners of tea.

Henry Fielding,
Love in Several Masques, 1728

I MET MARK BEAMISH at the Travellers Club in London, just after I moved to England. The president of the club, knowing my background in Ceylon, introduced the two of us. We sat together at a small dinner following a speech by the former governor of Hong Kong. This was in 1997, and Britain had only just given up control of her colony to the Chinese. We soon discovered that we had much in common: Ceylon, the world of tea planting, and colonial life in general. Beamish had read my autobiographical book, *The Man-Eater of Punanai*, which he much enjoyed. He said he loved Ceylon and had fond memories of the island. But unfortunately Sri Lanka had ruined him. Then he told me his story – some of it at dinner, the rest in the club's library over coffee and brandy.

He was then, I would guess, in his late seventies, and both broad and stout, easy-going, obviously used to good living. One could immediately see that he would have been quite a popular figure among the up-country planters in Ceylon. He told me that he had promised himself that he would retire on his fiftieth birthday.

In 1945, when he was twenty, he had left England and gone out to Ceylon as a 'creeper', that is an apprentice, for Carsons, probably the best tea management company in Ceylon; and over the next thirty years had worked his way up to become 'Periya Dorai' – the senior planter – at Nemwood, one of the largest and most productive tea estates near Nuwara Eliya. He had never married, but planned to settle down after he retired to Somerset, somewhere near Taunton, where he had gone to school. He was good at cricket at school, in fact got a full colour, and planned to spend a great deal of his time at the Somerset County Cricket Club supporting the county team. In preparation, he had become a member.

And then 1975 rolled around – the year he planned to retire. He would turn fifty on 5 December that year. By now he was not only the senior planter on the Nemwood Estate but also one of the partners in the very profitable Land's End Tea Company, which owned Nemwood and two other smaller estates near Horton Plains. Nearly everything he had was invested in this company and he was hoping to make enough money to retire from the sale of his interest. Life in tea had been lonely, but on the whole he had been contented. Like other British planters he had spent many a pleasant evening in Nuwara Eliya's Hill Club – an exclusive watering hole. The lives of most Hill Club members were devoted to tea.

Now tea, a plant of the *Camellia* family, requires sun and rain and grows mainly in the south-west of the island of Ceylon – by 1975, Sri Lanka. High-grown tea grows on hill slopes at altitudes up to nearly 6,500 feet and is considered to be the best quality. Elevations between 1,500 and 3,200 feet are categorized as mid-country, those below 1,500 feet as low-country. High-grown tea in the early 1970s accounted for a little over a quarter of the total output of Sri Lanka, low-country tea over half. Beamish concentrated on the high-grown variety. High-grown seemed a safe investment – much safer than coffee. Every tea planter knew that tea cultivation took off only after a blight started to destroy the coffee plantations, which until the 1870s had been Ceylon's main industry.

In the middle of the year, Beamish advised the other partners of the Land's End Company of his intention to sell up. Not surprisingly, there were many prospective buyers. His fellow directors had determined that the price for his holding would be set on the morning of his birthday at a meeting scheduled at the Hill Club, followed by a celebratory lunch.

But then, on 17 October, the Bandaranaike government dropped a bombshell on the tea industry. It amended the Land Reform Law, so that all the tea plantations were effectively nationalized. The management of the estates would be entrusted to two large state-run companies. It was an enormous shock to the industry, without precedent in the history of the country. Many private owners of estates, both foreign and local, at first had absolutely no idea what valuation the government would put on their holdings. The entire industry was in complete disarray. In the end the government unilaterally decided to pay £75, or about Rs.1,125, per acre – an unbelievably low price. Beamish had paid more than seven times that figure for his interest in the Company, and had borrowed heavily to do so. He was expecting to get as much as Rs.12,000 when he sold his shares – which would certainly have given him enough money to retire. As it was, he was now deeply in debt, with no job, and little or no chance of paying back the money he had borrowed from the Chartered Bank in Colombo. The government gave him thirty days to vacate the estate bungalow with all his personal possessions. It was a bitter blow. Like most other European planters, Beamish had no choice but to return to England, taking with him what little he had.

He left Colombo two days after his birthday in December on a P&O liner which took three weeks to dock in Southampton. His married sister, who had paid for his ticket, met him when he arrived and took him to her cottage in Berkshire. Eventually, he got a job planting in south India. But he spent most of his life repaying debts and struggling to make ends meet.

I felt sorry for Beamish. I told him that our family too had a rough time after Ceylon was given its independence in 1948. We had virtually to start over again in England, and eventually in Canada. Then

I made signs that it was time to leave because it was past eleven o'clock. But Beamish urged me to stay after the others had left and said their good-byes.

'I know this is a sad story,' he said, 'but I wanted you to stay because it isn't the whole story. I have never told anyone else what I am about to tell you. But having read your book about the Punanai leopard, I know that you are fascinated by local hearsay and superstition. In fact, you may understand what happened to me more than I do.

'I told you I never married but the truth is that for much of the time I was running Nemwood – I suppose for the best part of ten years – I had a Tamil girl as a mistress. She was beautiful and only sixteen years old when I hired her as a servant to help my cook in the kitchen. However, over time she was gradually given the responsibility for looking after my clothes, bringing me my morning tea and that sort of thing. Well, one thing led to another, when planters were left on their own for endless days and nights away from civilization, and one morning when she brought me my tea we became lovers. I think both of us knew what we were doing. She spoke very little English, but I have never felt the need for much conversation. I don't think the other servants knew what was going on for several months, but inevitably they found out; there are few secrets kept in an isolated planter's bungalow on a tea estate. Nothing is said, but everything is noticed. I never discussed her with any of my employees and certainly never with any of my fellow planters at the Hill Club. Probably they would have frowned on this kind of a relationship for a senior planter.

'Anyway, everyone including my servants knew in 1975 that I would be retiring and leaving Ceylon at the end of the year. And I suppose they all knew that my money was tied up in the estate and the Land's End Tea Company. Of course they couldn't possibly have known the details, but they might, perfectly reasonably, have expected that I would treat them generously for all the years they had spent looking after me. Well, one evening early in the year my little Tamil friend came to me and in her broken English asked me whether I was leaving the estate and leaving the country at the end of the year. It was a direct question and I took her to mean she was inquiring what was to become of her. So I explained that she would be well looked after. I would get her a job and give her enough money so that she could be independent and not have to work if she didn't want to. But then I realized that this wasn't at all what she was getting at. Somehow, she managed to get across to me, if I was going to leave the estate, I should get out now. Immediately. She was quite insistent and was soon in a terrible state. I couldn't calm her down. I presumed that she felt something terrible was going to happen to her, so I continued to assure her that everything was safe and she would be looked after. On several later occasions during the year she urged me to leave everything immediately. It was of course impossible, and she must have known this after so many years of our being together. Just a few months later, of course, the awful nationalization news broke. I couldn't help but remember her anguished pleas. I am sure now that she was not at all concerned with herself: she was warning me of a coming catastrophe.'

'But how could she possibly have known?' I asked.

'She couldn't possibly have known. Not about the nationalization anyway. But you know these people. They are brilliantly intuitive and rely on *huniangs* and spells, demonology and witchcraft, *vederalas*, astrology and all kinds of other things we Westerners don't understand. She definitely knew that as far as we two were concerned, and I suppose she herself, some dreadful event was about to happen – and it did. I've never been able to put her words out of my mind. Life would have been a lot different for me if I had paid some attention to her. It's a funny old world, isn't it?'

THE DEVIL BIRD

The Sinhalese regard the Devil Bird with
horror, and its scream by night in the vicinity
of a village is bewailed as the harbinger of
impending calamity.

Sir James Emerson,
Tennent in Ceylon: An Account of the Island,
Physical, Historical, and Topographical, 1859

IT WAS MY FATHER who first warned me about the devil bird. This was when we were living in Kuttapitiya, the tea estate where we children grew up, wild and carefree. More than any other member of the family, I shared with my father a love of the outdoors and wildlife; it was a bond he encouraged on our walks around the estate and on holidays. 'Christopher, do you want to come?' he would yell as he set off on an estate inspection. I accompanied him, partly because I loved him so much and partly because he would be angry if I didn't go. As we walked, he taught me about history, about nature and about confidence, and always encouraged me in any interest I had, whether it was in birds or athletics or boating. I particularly remember the year when the two of us went on a trip around the island. I was twelve, so this must have been in 1946. The trip was probably the highlight of my life until then; it was certainly the last thing my father and I did together before he sent me away to England. Our journey took us by car, with a driver from the estate, first down to the Yala Game Reserve on the south-east coast, and then north to the ancient cities of Sigiriya,

Anuradhapura and Polonnaruwa. But at no point did we encounter a devil bird.

As my father explained, the devil bird is rarely seen. In fact, there is still a debate about what it is. Suggestions have included a highland nightjar and a spot-bellied eagle owl, but the best evidence favours the forest eagle owl (*Huhua nipalensis*) in up-country areas, or the hawk-eagles and the crested honey buzzard (*Pernis ptilorhynchus ruficollis*) in lowland jungles.

Whatever its ornithological identity, the Sinhalese superstition is that the cry of the devil bird is an omen of death. According to an ancient legend, there was once a jealous husband who suspected his wife of infidelity. During her absence he murdered their child and made a curry from the corpse. He served it to his wife, who ate it, until she found the baby's finger on her plate. Mad with grief and disgust, she fled into the jungle and killed herself, but the gods transformed her into a bird, the devil bird, which still horrifies the world with its hysterical screams, like the wail of the Irish banshee. The cry of the devil bird has been compared to the sound of a baby being strangled, a boy being tortured, or a lost child whose wailings break off into a pitiful choking sob.

R. L. Spittel found a variation of the myth in the folklore of the Veddas, the earliest inhabitants of Ceylon. A Vedda and his son, Koa, were out hunting for three days without success. They were both ravenous. The father told his son to kindle a fire and, when it was burning, he thrust Koa into it, roasted him, and ate some of the flesh. Then he took part of the meat to his wife, who cooked it. But while sharing it out she suddenly became aware that it was her son's flesh. 'Digging the handle of the spoon into her head, she screamed "Koa," fled into the forest and died. And now, as the crested *Ulama*, she makes the midnight jungle echo with that wail.'

Even stranger are the tales told by a man named Shelley Crozier. He was an apprentice with the railways in the 1920s, who went hunting on three occasions with three different friends to the same waterhole in the remote Eastern Province of Ceylon. On each occasion he heard the devil bird cry under a full moon.

The first visit was with Phillip, a fellow apprentice. 'Here was a whitish brown bird with a hooked beak and about the size of a hawk, craning its neck to get a better look at us', Crozier reported. 'When exactly opposite my friend, it stretched its neck forward, puffed its neck feathers out, and then shattered the silence with its deadly scream. Screaming and shaking its head up and down, as though it was abusing my friend, it shut up and was about to fly off when I shot it a bare foot away from the point of my gun. My friend was sweating from every pore of his body, and by the light of the moon, he looked as pale as death.'

'I am not long for this world', Phillip prophesied. At dawn, when he saw the dead bird, he shouted: 'For God's sake take me from here.' Five days later, Phillip was struck by a bus. 'The curse of the devil bird', he said to Crozier in the hospital, and died.

The next year, Crozier visited the same waterhole with another friend, who had been warned about the bird. They heard the horrible scream and the bird flew out of the night and dropped a chameleon onto his friend's lap. He laughed the incident off, but four days later he became ill and was sent to hospital. 'Devil bird', he whispered to Crozier, and died.

The following year, Crozier was back in exactly the same place with yet another friend, Noel. He, too, had been warned about the bird, but insisted on making the trip. 'Devil or angel, I stay', Noel said bravely at first. But as the darkness came, his courage departed. 'Let's can this damned shoot and get out of here, even if we have to get lost!' he said. But they didn't go, nor did they sleep. Then the scream was heard. 'I am bloody sorry I came', said Noel. An hour later, there was another scream, and the bird flew low over Noel's head. Two weeks later, he too was dead.

A bit late in the day, Crozier decided not to tempt fate any further. 'I vowed that I would never again take a friend to that place as long as I lived.'

All of these stories of the devil bird, and the warnings given me as a child, swirled around my head when I returned to Sri Lanka after four decades away from the island, to research *The Man-Eater of Punanai*. With my friends Childers Jayawardena and Lakshman 'Lucky' Senatilleke, I planned to retrace the last trip I had made with my father, heading first to Yala, then to the ancient cities, and eventually to Punanai. Somewhere along the way I hoped, perhaps unwisely, to hear a devil bird.

It was an unsettled time for the country. Throughout the autumn and winter of 1989, as I was getting ready to return, the newspapers were full of stories about the island's civil war. Government troops were clashing with rebels, bombs were exploding in markets and buses, and innocent people were getting killed. The country was virtually a powder keg. We knew we might get caught in the cross-fire between warring factions, but our determination to succeed in our eight-week research safari overrode all other considerations. From Colombo we headed for Galle; then Hambantota and the flat, dry, yellow-brown scrubland that I love so much; and then, via Tissamaharama, to the arid and sandy terrain that makes up the four hundred square miles of the Yala Game Reserve. This was going to be our home for the first four weeks.

We searched for leopards, of course, spending the first few days in the Talgasmankada bungalow, a small building, just a couple of rooms and an L-shaped verandah, on the bank of the Menik River. 'Talgasmankada' means 'the crossing where the *tal* trees are'. The bungalow was almost bare of furnishings and had no electricity and only a little water, but it was wonderfully shaded by its huge deciduous trees. The only telephone connection was at Tissamaharama, forty miles distant. Every few days we had to go out for fresh food.

Other than that, news of fighting in the area or reports of murders reached us only by word of mouth. After a day or two we began to clear our minds, to the point that all we really cared about was having a pair of dry shoes, a hat against the sun, and a dose of mosquito repellent.

We slept on the verandah. The rooms were too hot for sleeping, so a row of cots was placed along the gallery facing the river. Lucky and Childers quietly chose cots in the centre, I noticed, leaving me with the first cot a wild animal would come to on its nocturnal prowl! But we all got used to our positions, including the park trackers. The days were long, patiently tracking leopards and interviewing people; and I was really getting into the rhythm of the research, eager to begin each new day. The nights, lit only by kerosene lamps, were magical. For three nights in a row we slept well in a cool breeze with few mosquitoes. Sometimes I was awakened by a sound and shone my flashlight into the eerie blackness, catching the inquisitive eyes of deer, hares and squirrels. We got used to occasional raucous cries of peacocks, and more rarely the sawing rasp of a leopard coming from across the river.

Then, on the fourth night, there was a disturbance. The jungle noises were louder, and neither Childers nor Lucky seemed able to settle down. Deep in the night a shot rang out. It came from the other side of the river, perhaps a mile away. Terrorists? I could tell that the others were awake, but nobody moved or said a word. The crack of the rifle shot had set off a chorus of jungle shrieks, led by the peacocks and a couple of langurs; amid all this commotion, suddenly I heard the notorious blood-curdling scream, which really sounded as if a baby was being strangled. None of us made the least noise. I lay wide awake for a quite a while, until at last the jungle quietened down and I was able to drop into a fitful sleep.

The morning brought a change of plan that seemed like another ill omen. Originally, I had intended to spend five days in

Talgasmankada, go off to another part of the park for some days, then return for five more days. Now, we were instructed to go immediately to the Patanangala bungalow on the coast. Childers, a former game warden, explained that this would allow him to pursue his research on sea turtles, but I suspected that he and Lucky had decided that it would be safer to move away from the Talgasmankada bungalow. A couple of years before this, the bungalow had been burned to the ground, and it was now located on the main escape route for terrorists trying to flee north from the coast into the interior of the island. The fighting was apparently getting closer. Wanniarachchi, one of the trackers, was strangely quiet and seemed very edgy.

We packed quickly before having a rapid breakfast, piled into the jeeps, and left Talgasmankada shortly after sunrise. I was in one jeep with Lucky, Wanniarachchi and Raja, our driver. Childers followed in the other with its driver, the other tracker and our bags. We headed along the track towards Patanangala. The jungle seemed very still.

We were just about to turn left down the Patanangala road to the sea when Wanniarachchi, silent until now, burst into a stream of agitated Sinhalese, talking mainly to Lucky but also to Raja, who stopped the jeep abruptly, letting Childers pass us and turn his jeep towards the Patanangala bungalow. Lucky himself seemed agitated, looking from Wanniarachchi to Raja and back again. No one spoke for a minute or so, then Lucky looked at me and said: 'Chris, we must go to Kataragama immediately. This is important. Wanniarachchi's daughter has a baby girl and he is worried she may be sick. I think the devil bird is responsible. It's the first time Wanniarachchi's ever heard its cry.' He fell silent. 'Shall I drop you off at the bungalow and then go with Wanniarachchi to Kataragama and come back a bit later?' Lucky asked.

'No,' I said, 'we must all go. Let's go quickly to the bungalow, tell Childers, and then head for Kataragama. If the baby is ill we must do what we can right away.'

It took a few minutes to get to the Patanangala bungalow and a few more to explain the problem to Childers, then we turned around and drove back to the Talgasmankada road, reached the Katagamuwa entrance to the park, and drove the six miles to Kataragama. The path to the sacred site that has brought pilgrims of all faiths through the jungle for hundreds of years was now an easily drivable red gravel road, yet thousands still walk the route to Kataragama through 'God's country', chanting 'Haro Hara'. Everyone in our jeep was silent, serious, intent.

The last stretch took us almost into the town of Kataragama, before Wanniarachchi directed Raja to turn left down Vallimathagama Road to find a thatched wattle-and-daub hut at the end of the road. Both Wanniarachchi and Lucky got out immediately. I stayed in the jeep with Raja. Wanniarachchi didn't knock, but simply opened the door. We saw his daughter, quite unconcerned, greet him. But after a burst of conversation in Sinhalese, a horrified expression appeared on her face, and both she and Wanniarachchi disappeared into the house leaving the door open. I could see them hurrying down a corridor leading to a far corner of the dwelling. Lucky stayed outside the house smoking and fidgeting nervously. We said nothing to each other, fearing the worst.

After eight, maybe nine, minutes, they reappeared with the two-year-old daughter in her mother's arms. Wanniarachchi's granddaughter seemed to be perfectly alright, but it was obvious from their faces that he and his daughter were still very upset. They continued to talk seriously for some time before Lucky and the tracker climbed back into the jeep. Lucky said nothing to me, and I decided to keep quiet.

Just as we turned off the highway into Yala, Lucky turned his head and said: 'You know, Chris, I am not a particularly superstitious man, and I think I have heard the devil bird a few times in my life. But Wanniarachchi has not, and last night must have triggered something in his mind. He was very nervous, and convinced that something terrible had happened to his granddaughter. That's why he insisted on going to Kataragama right away. He wouldn't have asked normally, because he knows how important this work you are doing is to you. But he was convinced that a curse had been thrown on his family and particularly on his daughter. The amazing thing is, he may have been right. And we may have got there only just in time. The little girl was in her room asleep, but when Wanniarachchi and his daughter went to her they found her head stuck between the bars of her cot. Anything might have happened. They had an awful time getting the child's head free. Wanniarachchi's daughter was in a terrible state. It's a lucky thing that we came right away. I don't know about this devil bird but there are so many stories and so many warnings that it is no wonder people are terrified when they hear the bird scream.'

We drove the rest of the way to our park bungalow in complete silence.

A WHITE CROW

*Although I have seen nothing but black crows in
my life, it doesn't mean that there's no such thing
as a white crow. Both for a philosopher and for
a scientist it can be important not to reject the
possibility of finding a white crow.*

Jostein Gaarder,
Sophie's World, 1995

I THINK THE STRANGEST afternoon I have ever spent in Colombo
was my last meeting with the late president of Sri Lanka, J. R.
Jayawardene. A remarkable politician with an authoritative presence,
he was the island's first executive president from 1978 to 1989, having
masterminded the change of the country's constitution to a Gaullist
system. While president, he wielded immense power, though sometimes for questionable motives. His failure to prevent Sinhalese mobs
from attacking Tamils in a frenzy of ethnic violence in July 1983
undoubtedly fuelled the separatist struggle of militant Tamil groups
in Sri Lanka and the emigration of many Tamil families. This led to
the intervention of India's peace-keeping force on his country's soil
in 1987. Despite Jayawardene's considerable efforts at peace-making,
Sri Lanka's separatist struggle intensified, not diminished, during his
period as president.

I remember him as a superb raconteur. Over tea at his home in
Ward Place, he held me enthralled with his recollections of Queen
Elizabeth II's visit to Sri Lanka in 1981. 'How would you like your
people to see me?' the queen asked the president. 'I think they would

like to see you with your crown on, Your Majesty', Jayawardene replied. 'I'm sorry, Mr President, but I don't travel with my crown', the queen apologized. Later, the queen told him that her most embarrassing moment as queen had been in Uganda during a state visit in 1954 when, during a private and intimate moment, four hundred school children had burst into 'God Save the Queen'.

He was also a student of history, and this was what brought us together in 1993, three years before he died at the age of ninety. I was in Sri Lanka to help the historian Hendrik Hooft publish his epic biography *Patriot and Patrician*, which followed the life in Holland and Ceylon of our ancestors Hendrik Hooft and Pieter Ondaatje. In the 1780s, Hooft and Ondaatje were champions of a popular movement that brought the Dutch Republic the first democratically elected government in Europe, a few years before the French Revolution.

But right now I have less to say about President Jayawardene's politics and intellect than about the birds in his garden. As anyone knows who has visited one of the spacious houses that line the avenue of Colombo's Ward Place, where many high-ranking politicians and officials have their residences, the area's trees, gardens and pavements abound in armies of noisy crows. They are large birds, over a foot long, with heavy pointed bills and powerful legs. Omnivorous, they eat fruit, large insects, small vertebrates, as well as other birds' eggs and young. In my experience, they are extremely intelligent, gregarious, and black with a very slight metallic sheen.

Hence, it was not surprising that as 'Henk' Hooft and I were driven with the former president in his limousine through the guarded gates to the portico of his house, we noticed a number of crows busily going about their activities in his garden. What was surprising to us was that one crow was entirely white, except for its pink legs and a light grey beak. This unique-looking crow seemed to be bossing the activities of the other crows.

Intent on listening to the former president, I said nothing about the peculiar sight until much later in the afternoon after we had had sandwiches and tea and were thinking of leaving. At this point, Jayawardene moved to the window overlooking the garden and himself seemed engrossed in watching the crows. I seized my moment, stood next to him and asked about the white crow. His long and enigmatic face was pensive for a considerable time. Then he looked at me and said with unexpected seriousness: 'I think we had better sit down again.'

Placing himself in an armchair away from the window, he asked us: 'What do you know about Meredith Foster? Do you remember, a few years ago, the British press announced the disappearance of this English reporter who came to Sri Lanka in the mid-1980s to cover the violence against the Tamil minority? It was a terrible time for us, and particularly difficult for me because I had to make some very tough decisions. Not everything worked, even with the help of the Indian peace-keeping force. In fact, the strained relationship between the Sinhalese and Tamil population got worse with the unpopular Indian involvement.'

I let him talk. 'Anyway, Miss Foster's reports – and I call her Miss Foster even though she had a husband in England – received world-wide attention for a while, particularly in the Western world. She was a good writer, with a better-than-average understanding of a compli-cated political situation, and took some quite extraordinary risks to get her stories – sometimes actually going to the battle fronts and war zones where reporters were definitely not allowed. She made a name for herself overseas, but also here in Colombo where she was based and where she spent most of her time when she was not in the field. Her husband did visit her occasionally at first, but she seemed to have made a permanent home for herself in the Barnes Place area, not far from here. I suppose she had been living there for six or seven years when she suddenly went missing, supposedly on one of her more dangerous reporting missions. There was real consternation because both the Tamil Tigers and the Sri Lankan army had taken great pains to advise and protect foreign journalists, knowing full well the bad press they would get if a Western reporter were hurt or killed. For a long time there was confusion as to Miss Foster's whereabouts and her reporting mission. No body was ever found. And then, after a few months with no further news of her, the situation died down and the press coverage basically stopped.'

I did recall the reports in England about the disappearance of an English reporter in Sri Lanka. It had caused quite a stir at the time, as he said; but I chose to say nothing, as the former president seemed anxious to continue with his story.

'Well, what very few people outside the government knew was that Meredith Foster, a good-looking blonde in her mid-thirties, was having rather a serious affair with a high-ranking minister, who had his house in this area. The relationship was an embarrassment for all of us, but no action was taken, although the minister in question – himself a married man – was warned several times about the dangers of the compromising relationship. The situation was further complicated because the minister's wife was related to the Bandaranaike family and we knew she was understandably in a high state of anxiety about her husband. Most of the cabinet knew there would be trouble at some point.'

Now Jayawardene seemed to change tack. 'Here I need to ask you a fairly personal question. Do either of you know anything about demonology and witchcraft?' I decided to shake my head, as did Henk, without taking our eyes off his face. He was clearly eager to speak.

'Sri Lanka, together with Haiti and South Africa, is known to be among the most sophisticated countries in the practice of demon worship. Superstition, coupled with the worship of gods and demons, as well as Buddhism, has had an extraordinary degree of

influence on the minds of the Sinhalese. Even respected historians and writers such as Robert Knox in the seventeenth century, and more recently Sir James Emerson Tennent, have researched and written on the subject. Curiously, Buddhism acknowledges the probable existence of demons and tolerates demon worship, even if it does not openly encourage it. A Sinhalese demon is himself a being subject to death, like all other beings recognized by Buddhism, although that event may in some instances take place only at the end of some tens of thousands of years. This difference arises from the Buddhist doctrine that there is no state of perpetual existence for any being; that happiness or misery can never be perpetual; and that the rewards or punishments for the actions of one life will be reaped in one or more states of existence afterwards and then come to an end. Thus, mere obedience to a demon does not necessitate any disobedience to one's religion.

'The priests of demonism are styled *yakaduras, yakdessas,* or more commonly *cattadiyas,* and there is scarcely a village in the island that does not boast of at least one. So it is not that surprising that when someone gets into trouble, or is involved in a relationship or situation which cannot be resolved in a normal way, they put themselves in the hands of a village *cattadiya.* These people have the means to call on one of the demons, who are invisible but have the power to make themselves visible, generally in some other shape, often that of beasts, or of men, or of women. You must understand that *cattadiyas* receive no particular respect from anyone as the Buddhist priest does. The profession of *cattadiya* is looked upon as an ordinary calling, like a shopkeeper or a boatman. There is nothing sacred about him, and his main job is to cure or inflict diseases and achieve other tasks via the agency of demons.

'There are a great number of these demons and they are said to have enormous influence over life, death, disease, health and love. However, the number of those who are worshipped does not exceed fifty or sixty. Worship is a complicated business involving various kinds of charms, the object of which is to bind a demon in a certain manner so as to make it an obedient slave of its worshipper. There are many learned books and letters on the subject, most of which have not been translated from Sinhala.

'Among the demons is Baddracali, whose assistance is sought for winning lawsuits and for subduing enemies and rivals of any kind. Baddracali would have been a suitable demon for the wife of the government minister to have appealed to against her English rival, with the help of her *cattadiya* in her home village close to Kandy. However, discreet enquiries suggested that the lady in question actually appealed to Bahirawa Yakseya, another female demon, generally feared for being able to inflict diseases on women. Bahirawa Yakseya is very well known around the giant hill, Bahirawa Canda, overlooking one side of the city of Kandy, near the wife's village. Residents of the Kandy region are steeped in the folklore of Bahirawa Yakseya. Most famously, the demon helped an early queen of Kandy, who had miscarried several times. Through the agency of a *cattadiya*, Bahirawa Yakseya stated that she would not remove her malign influence over the queen unless an annual sacrifice of a young virgin was made to her on the summit of Bahirawa Canda. To be precise, a stake had to be driven into the ground on the summit of Bahirawa Canda; the girl tied to it with jungle creepers; flowers and boiled rice placed close by on an altar constructed for the purpose; and certain invocations and incantations pronounced. The girl herself was not to be killed by the worshipper. But as a rule, in such sacrifices the following morning the girl would be found dead. When the king of Kandy agreed to Bahirawa Yakseya's demand, and had the sacrifice performed, several children were born to his young wife.

'I say "as a rule," because Bahirawa Yakseya, though she is said to have considerable powers over disease, does not have any direct power over death. The escape of the virgin from death is therefore possible – either by reincarnation, where she can choose to take the form of a human in another life at another time, or by immediate transformation into an animal or bird of the demon's choosing and approval.

'Rumour has it that the minister's wife was told by her *cattadiya* that in order to rid herself of Meredith Foster and save her marriage, she must sacrifice her rival in the same way that the sacrifices were made for the queen of Kandy. Thus it was, we suspected, that Foster was kidnapped during one of her many reporting assignments, taken to Bahirawa Canda in Kandy and tied to the sacrificial stake. But since no body was ever found, she most probably escaped death.

'Nobody really knows what happened. But I think there may be a clue. This unique white crow – which is, by the way, a female crow – appeared in Ward Place at almost exactly the same time that Meredith Foster disappeared. No one talks about it much because Sri Lankans, as I've explained, are extremely superstitious and fear reprisals from demons if they question their orders. Of course people sometimes come, with official permission, to see the albino bird, but they say nothing. Often it flies off to other gardens in the area, but everyone around here is very careful not to disturb or frighten it in any way, and certainly not to harm it. Eventually it always returns here.'

After the perplexing story was over, Henk Hooft and I stared at the former president in disbelief. We said nothing. I was just about to make our excuses and leave, when there was a strange sound from the window: a persistent tapping. The sight disconcerted us, to say the very least. We could see the white crow was outside on the window sill, where it appeared to be tapping out a message in some sort of code.

Jayawardene, completely unfazed, got up, walked purposefully to the window and opened it. Immediately the white crow flew into the drawing room, circled briefly around the centre, and then alighted on the former president's shoulder, as if she knew exactly what was expected of her. I was about to say something when I saw him look at me with a threatening scowl. We stared at each other for a few moments. He said nothing. Nothing needed to be said. Then his face relaxed, and with a half-apologetic smile he gave a shrug, taking care not to disturb the remarkably possessive bird.

THE HUMAN LEOPARD SOCIETY

*People who live in towns can hardly realise how
persistent and violent are the desires of those who live
in villages like Beddagama. In many ways, and in this
beyond all others, they are very near to the animals;
in fact, in this they are more brutal than the brutes;
that, while the animals have their seasons, man alone
is perpetually dominated by his desires.*

Leonard Woolf,
The Village in the Jungle, 1913

SOMETIMES I HAVE FOUND that while searching for information
on one event, I come across an even more extraordinary set of facts
about something completely different. This is what happened to me
after drafting the conclusion to my book *Woolf in Ceylon*.

When I left Sri Lanka in March 2004, I left behind some unfin-
ished Woolf business. Was there, or was there not, a 'real' village in
the jungle that formed the basis of Woolf's *The Village in the Jungle*,
the masterful novel of Ceylon he published in 1913? There are some
strong resemblances between passages in Woolf's government diaries
and passages in the novel. While we were travelling in the arid
Hambantota district, villagers assured us that there was such a place
as Woolf's village, although everyone agreed that it was not called
Beddagama, the name of the village in the novel. So, in December
2004, I returned to Sri Lanka to see what, if anything, I could find
out about this mysterious village and the two murders that feature in
Woolf's novel. In Woolf's government diary, a double murder is

recorded as occurring in a village named Malasnegalwewa in the Magam Pattu jungle in December 1910. In the end, with persistence and some luck, we tracked down a resident of that area, Ajith Siriwardena, who showed us an original 1911 land grant to Don Bastyan Siriwardena of Malasnegalwewa in return for Rs. 75 'as security for the due performance of duties as police officer and divisional officer of Malasnegalwewa by the grantor'.

I was therefore satisfied that Woolf had based his novel on Malasnegalwewa and its violent events in 1910, elaborating his story from real events using his profound knowledge of the villages in the area. Certainly, the villagers of Malasnegalwewa accept the link between their village, a historical double murder, and the double murder in Beddagama in Woolf's novel.

But what really piqued my curiosity is that Ajith Siriwardena's uncle, A. D. Siripala, while we were having tea in his house waiting to photograph the land grant document for my book, alerted me to yet another, hardly discussed, strange death that took place in the Magam Pattu jungle a year or two after the events featured in *The Village in the Jungle*.

In this case, a youth, barely fourteen years old, had been found dead one morning in thick jungle. Deep incisions were seen on the boy's throat and on his chest, and part of his body above the left breast had been torn away. The gouges were almost certainly caused by the claws of a leopard, a predator that frequented Magam Pattu. The death was reported to the *vel-vidane*, the headman, of Migahajandura, the boy's village, who told the police. But the boy's father refused to allow the boy to be buried quickly, as is the custom in the tropics, because he did not believe the boy had been attacked by a leopard. He demanded an official examination of the boy's wounds by the local doctor. At the father's insistence, that evening the *vederala*, who had been summoned from Tissamaharama, examined the dead boy in the father's hut, watched by the police and a crowd of onlookers. He said nothing to the father and gave his medical opinion only to the *vel-vidane*. The following day, a bulletin was posted by the police in Sinhalese, and a report in English was sent to the government agent at Hambantota, Sydney Hay, who had succeeded Woolf in 1911.

Siripala, a balding, excitable village elder, seemed to have an amazing memory for the case. I asked him how he knew the facts in such detail. 'You will see, you will see', he said, and continued his story.

The doctor's findings declared that the boy's wounds had *not* been caused by a leopard's claws but by a claw-like metal instrument, which might be a knife. In his opinion, the boy's death had the appearance of being a ritual killing, but not of a kind he had seen or heard of. Naturally there was consternation among the villagers of Migahajandura; a police murder hunt was ordered; and the boy's body was viewed by the government agent, before being photographed and at last buried according to Buddhist custom.

Hay agreed with the doctor's forensic judgment. Immediately, he gave orders to the police to search for any person of African descent or who had spent some time on the African continent who might have been present in the area at the time of the murder. Clearly the government agent saw some connection between the murder and his personal experience in West Africa, where he had been posted before coming to Ceylon.

At first the search was fruitless. Then the police struck gold. They found a man from West Africa, Yagba Sawura, a sailor on a salt boat who had come to collect from the salt pans at Hambantota not long before and remained illegally in Magam Pattu. Under interrogation, Sawura let slip that he had once been a member of a proscribed West African society notorious to Hay for its ritual killings. After prolonged questioning by the police, the man confessed in the presence of the government agent to the murder of the young boy and revealed the names of two other men who had assisted him in his gruesome enterprise. All three men were now charged with murder and three other boys, whose names had been given by Sawura, were called for questioning as witnesses.

I was about to ask Siripala a question about this intriguing African connection, but he gesticulated wildly and continued with his gory tale.

The three boys gave evidence during the court proceedings in Hambantota, presided over by the government agent as judge. They had been abducted while out walking on a path and taken deep into the Magam Pattu jungle, along with the victim. There one of the accused men ordered the four boys to clear a small area and build a simple grass hut. Here the boys slept for two nights without any kind of protection against the jungle, except for that of their captors. On the second morning, before daybreak, the three boys were awakened by a noise and saw two of the accused men dragging the victim out of the hut, while a third man stood watching, his face masked by a leopard skin draped over the top of his head and hanging down his back. Petrified, the three boys started to scream and the two assistants ran away, leaving the fourth boy alone with Sawura. Eventually, the three boys escaped and managed to make their way out of the jungle to their village, where they said they had got lost in the jungle and gave a garbled report of having seen a dead body. They said nothing about their own capture, or of the three men, for fear of reprisals from the accused. Although the boys were severely reprimanded by the judge for not having told the whole story at the time, after the court hearing they were allowed to go home with their parents.

'How,' I asked Siripala, 'did the government agent know that the murderer was from West Africa?' Apparently the combination of claw marks and the tearing of the left breast had alerted Hay. During his time in Sierra Leone, everyone knew of the long tradition of human cannibalism. The first reports of 'human leopards' had appeared more recently, only two or three decades earlier. Ritual killers dressed as leopards would cut flesh from the left breast of their victims and distribute it to members of their society. Such ritual cannibalism was supposed to strengthen both the members of the society and their tribe. There was a belief among certain tribes, the Temnes in particular, that by such witchcraft a man could turn himself into a leopard, and in that form could injure an enemy. Hay had seen a photograph, published by an American missionary society, of the skin of a large leopard with iron claws that had once belonged to a witch doctor who had used it to satisfy his craving. Through his own acquaintance with the Mende tribe, Hay also suspected that human leopard cannibalism was not a longstanding tradition and was probably no more than half a century old – hence the fact that reports of it had reached European ears only in the late nineteenth century. After some time, the government of Sierra Leone decided that exceptional legislation was necessary and passed the Human Leopard Society Ordinance of 1895, which forbade the possession of three things: a leopard skin shaped so as to make a man wearing it resemble a leopard; a five-pronged knife or claw; and a native medicine known as *borfima* made of human fat and blood.

Again and again, Siripala repeated what an extraordinary coincidence it was that the government agent in charge of this particular murder in Ceylon happened to be aware of the human leopard society in Sierra Leone. Entirely because of this coincidence, Sawura was sentenced to death by hanging, and his two so-called assistants to long terms of imprisonment.

'How do you know this in such detail?' I asked him once more. 'It is no secret', he said. 'I have been told this story by my father many, many times. You see, my father was one of the boys who were abducted and witnessed the ritual murder in the Magam Pattu jungle. He often told me that he was very lucky indeed not to have been the murderer's chosen victim.'

LEOPARD IN THE
AFTERNOON

Come with me and I will find what you are looking for. In the shadow of the yellow fever tree you will find beauty that you cannot touch, an image you can capture but not possess; and life you can protect but still destroy. After that you can dance to the music of tomorrow.

Joshua Mbowe,
safari guide, Tanzania

FOR THE FIRST FEW moments after I climbed back into the Land Rover with Joshua and started winding through the streets of Arusha, I wondered if the idea was not sheer madness. But as we hit the dusty red roads and moved out into the plains of Tanzania I knew I had made the right decision. Even if it seemed stupid and irresponsible, the effort was worth making, whether it paid off or not.

The journey was dusty, hot, uncomfortable. We could stop halfway and find some kind of lodging somewhere or try to get all the way to Seronera in one go. Joshua was keen to press on. He knew that the success of our crazy venture depended on him, and the Land Rover took a beating. It is a rule in the Serengeti Park that you cannot enter after sunset, so I understood why he was driving so fast. We had tried, unsuccessfully, to talk our way into the Ngorongoro Wildlife Lodge en route, and so we had to get at least to the Serengeti Park gate before six o'clock. We made it, but only just, and from there we wound across the plains, through the dramatic rock outcroppings, past the giant Simba Kopje, which towered a hundred feet above us, and eventually reached Seronera as darkness was falling.

Joshua seemed to know exactly what he was doing. We drove through the forks of the Seronera River to a very secluded site under an acacia tree. In almost complete silence we pitched the two small tents by the light of a bulb wired to the Land Rover's battery. After dinner Joshua told me that camping here was actually illegal: it was not a recognized site. He also told me he had camped here once before – with three nurses. They had all slept in one tent on the first night but one of them preferred to be alone on the second. She spent a fairly hectic night while an inquisitive male lion settled noisily next to her tent. His grunts and coughs terrified the poor woman; she got no sleep. It was the last time, said Joshua, that she tried sleeping alone.

A freak thunderstorm hit Seronera that night, a dramatic down-pour with sheet lightning that started just before midnight and lasted for the best part of an hour. Then about two hours later there was another downpour. It stopped quite suddenly and was followed by the noise of lions roaring all around the camp. We kept quiet and I lay awake listening as the deep, guttural sounds came closer. This nerve-racking experience continued for an hour. Then, just by Joshua's tent a few feet away, I heard a single, ear-splitting roar and a scraping and flapping against his tent. Joshua screamed. I thought the lion had attacked him but in fact he was trying to scare the beast away. A few seconds later I heard the same scraping sound – but this time against my own tent, a few inches from my head. The lion bumped against the tent pole and rubbed itself against the canvas, slinking around it. I didn't have the faintest idea what to do, but Joshua shouted to me to keep very quiet!

Before we went to bed, he had moved the Land Rover from under the acacia, where our supplies were, to the door of his tent. It was a lucky move that may have saved us. He leaped into the vehicle, started the motor and turned the lights on. A lioness and her five cubs stood there; she was looking for food. As Joshua rammed the Land Rover towards them, the lioness made a stealthy get-away, clutching a plastic water container in her jaws.

At first light we saw what had happened. It was clear from the paw prints around Joshua's tent that the lioness really had tried to attack him. Her teeth had torn right through the wall of his tent. My tent, too, was surrounded by her large pug marks, while those of her cubs were scattered in the soft mud around. Joshua said that in future he would sleep in the vehicle in case something similar were to happen again. I didn't think it was possible for both lightning and lions to strike twice in exactly the same place.

Shaken but undeterred, we headed straight for the Magadi Road, which runs close to the Seronera River, and spent the remainder of the morning cruising slowly up the valley looking for tracks and searching the trees. In the recently created pools by the river the usually sinister marabous looked like solemn deacons in prayer.

In this great open brown country, the landscape is broken by shallow, dried-up river valleys and by the yellow-barked fever trees, the flat-topped thorn acacias and the sausage trees. Yellow fever trees prefer areas near water, and early explorers frequently camped under them because of the certainty of water and shade. Naturally, areas of water are also favoured camping grounds for the malarial mosquito. To begin with, it was not known that mosquitoes carried the malaria parasite, but soon people concluded that anyone who camped beneath the fever tree was likely to contract malaria. An association was made between some mysterious power of the tree and the fever – hence its name.

It is in these trees that leopards usually spend most of the daylight hours. They lie in the lower branches about twelve or fourteen feet above ground and are extremely difficult to see. When they move, they do so under cover in long grass or dense thicket. The rougher the terrain the better, and the leopard's spotted skin provides perfect camouflage. Only in the afternoon can leopards be seen more easily, but searching for them is still like looking for a needle in a haystack. There are tails and limbs hanging down from the sausage and acacia trees all over Africa. However, most of these are imaginary; a real leopard's tail and limbs usually disappear as soon as it sees you.

We drove slowly along the valleys fruitlessly for nearly four hours, then had a makeshift lunch, standing dejectedly beside the Land Rover. After lunch we headed for the Seronera Wildlife Lodge where Joshua managed to get a small single room for me to dump my bags. It seemed a better bet than camping again in the lion range.

Joshua left to try and get hold of someone he knew in the village. I waited for a good hour, wondering what he was up to. He returned with a smiling, thick-set man in a green shirt. Martin Darabe, an Irangu tribesman, was a National Parks guide who had been at Seronera for a number of years. Quiet and good-humoured, he spoke little English but he knew the lie of the land. Joshua had explained everything to him. Martin said our best bet would be in the early evening, when leopards begin to get ready for the evening's hunting. But he thought it was worth going out now, even though it was the hottest part of the day. We had only a few hours to spare – the rest of this afternoon and perhaps part of the next morning – so we set out and tirelessly combed the fever trees up and down the winding valley.

Two hours later, we were still looking. I had almost given up hope when Martin said something quietly to Joshua in Swahili and Joshua said: 'I think der de leopard.' I peered at some acacias and saw nothing. The leopard wasn't in the first or the second group of trees but in a third, and very far away. How Martin saw it I haven't the faintest idea. It was the merest speck of a thing hanging down from a branch.

Joshua drove, for once carefully, keeping near cover in the rough terrain between us and the tree. I looked through my field glasses and a chill of excitement shivered down my spine. It was indeed a leopard. A female, about five years old, Martin estimated, sprawled along a branch with all four legs and tail dangling down like extra branches, and her head in a fork of the tree facing us.

She seemed lazy, and was evidently quite content to spend the greater part of the day in the shade. From the shelter of a neighbouring tree, at a distance of about thirty yards, I was able to take photograph after photograph of her. Then, when I had taken every picture I possibly could, I said: 'OK, Joshua. Now just go past her very slowly . . . Now turn left towards her . . . Just go under the branch.' Very disturbed, he said: 'I can't turn left.' He was afraid the leopard would jump into the open vehicle. Martin, too, was uneasy because we were breaking park regulations by driving off the track.

Joshua inched closer, while Martin warned him worriedly not to, looking around uneasily to make sure there was no one to see us. Breaking the law because of a crazy guy who wants to get closer and closer. They wanted to leave. I wanted to get closer.

I simply had to capture that moment, and I was willing to take any risk to do so. I was frightened, not of the leopard but that she would leave. I kept taking shots, then I was really close. I got out the 300mm lens and very nearly shot her in the face. I could almost feel her breath on my face. My eyes looked directly into hers in an uncanny moment of communication. Then I took the photograph I had been looking for. Everything came together: the light was right, the focus was right, the film was right.

And then, almost immediately, I knew I was outstaying my welcome. I truly was in danger. I had experienced one of the great thrills of my life, but it was time to go. We returned to Seronera in triumph.

THE SEMLIKI LEOPARD

*At the fourth hour it was quite a thin forest on
the left side of the Semliki, while to the right it was
a thick impervious and umbrageous tropic forest,
and suddenly we were on the bank of the Semliki.
At the point we touched the river it was sixty yards
wide with between a four- and five-knot current.*

Henry Morton Stanley,
In Darkest Africa, 1890

IN NOVEMBER 1996, nearing the end of a three-month journey
tracing the footsteps of the Victorian explorers of East Africa, I had
reached Kasese at the foot of the Ruwenzori Mountains in Uganda.
My quest was to unravel the mystery of the source of the River Nile,
which was designated as being Lake Victoria by John Hanning Speke
in 1858. Far from being just the source, Lake Victoria is in fact one of
the two great reservoirs of the Nile – the other being Lake Albert –
that are fed by two mighty rivers: the Kagera, which drains the
Burundi Highlands, and the Semliki, which drains the Ruwenzori
Mountains. I had travelled from Zanzibar to Bagamayo on the east
coast of Africa, and then to Tabora, Ujiji on Lake Tanganyika, Lake
Victoria and Ripon Falls, down the Victoria Nile to Murchison Falls
and the north end of Lake Albert, and eventually along the east coast
of Lake Albert to Fort Portal and Kasese, a sleepy mountain village in
the Ruwenzoris.

Exhausted, thirsty, and extremely hungry, we relaxed over some
Nile beers before dinner. We discussed the Ruwenzori Mountains at

length. Our initial plan was to spend six or eight days climbing some of their eastern slopes. I hoped to get above the cloud line, at least, to see the major peaks, so as to view the drainage system from that elevated position and come to whatever conclusions I could about it.

But the next day Kasese was in semi-chaos. Rebels – possibly from Zaire – had crossed the border only six miles west of the town and were moving down the Kazinga Channel, which runs between Lake George and Lake Edward. Armed men were everywhere, some in uniform but many not. So were refugees. Even without understanding a word of the language being spoken we could tell that everyone in Kasese was in a state of high alarm.

And so I took a decision to change course: instead of climbing I would round the southernmost tip of the Ruwenzori range until I reached the Semliki River on the border with Zaire. Few people ventured into this region, which is an equatorial forest: dense, muggy, luxuriant, mosquito and fly-infested swamp land. We would be almost totally alone there, or so we thought.

Descending into the Semliki Valley I noticed that the lower we went, the shorter the inhabitants seemed to be. Still further down, we started to see people carrying spears, then bows and arrows, and finally men with long beards. At last, almost at the foot of the mountains, lay the equatorial jungle we had expected, very humid and hot and dense, with massive trees soaring to great heights. We were right at the edge of the Semliki Forest Park, a virtually untouched tropical lowland forest, separated from the Ituri Forest of Zaire by the Semliki River.

We pitched camp in a small clearing completely surrounded by tall cane grass, some fifty yards from the rugged mountain road we had driven along. Walking further south into the jungle we found a small group of Bamba and Bakonjo people, often referred to as pygmies. However, nightfall was coming, so we headed back to camp, ate dinner and settled in for the night – I on my own in a small plastic tent about thirty yards away from Thad Petersen and our two Tanzanian bearers in a larger tent. Under the forest canopy the night was exceptionally dark, and I was lying on an uncomfortable ground-sheet, being bitten by minute insects known as bukukums (as I later discovered). The bites left painful welts, particularly around the eyes and ears. Sleeping was difficult. But eventually I dozed off.

Maybe only an hour or so later, there was the jarring sound of gunfire, yelling and shouting on the mountain road. I lay motionless, a virtual prisoner in my tent, thinking about the mayhem I had witnessed a few hours earlier in Kasese. What I had not realized was that during the day Laurent Kabila's troops had made their first attempt to overthrow the dictatorship of President Mobutu in Zaire. It was an ordeal to listen to the sounds, because I had no idea what to do. The nocturnal turmoil lasted for a good hour, then quietened down somewhat. I silently unzipped the front flap of the tent and shone my torch into the long grass on either side of the narrow path that led away from the clearing. Imagine my surprise when, instead of shadowy rebel soldiers, I caught sight of two bright orange eyes shining back at me from the edge of the clearing. From long experience I knew such eyes could belong only to a large cat, perhaps a leopard.

I shone my torch steadily at the eyes and saw a motionless figure, which was still gazing at me. Then, without moving its feet, the stealthy predator turned its head and looked down the narrow path towards the sound of the crowd on the mountain road. In the torch beam I recognized the tawny hide and rosettes of a full-grown female leopard, with a long twitching tail, staring at something I couldn't see in the distance. I remained rooted to the spot. But I kept shining my torch on the beast. After some long moments, perhaps even a minute, the leopardess slowly, soundlessly, moved away from the path into the centre of the clearing towards an invisible spot behind my tent, concealed from the road.

I dared not move or create a sound, but very slowly and silently crouched down again on my ground-sheet and shut off the torch. The sounds of the fleeing rebels seemed finally to be moving away, the danger becoming more distant. In due course, I heard only the forest noises, sharpened by my now-acute alertness. There was the occasional rustle of wind in the trees, the whir of cicadas, the drone of a persistent mosquito. And then I became aware of another sound. Right next to my tent. I strained my ears and there could be no mistake: I could hear a low guttural breathing, only a few feet away. Had the leopardess sought protection or cover from my tent, away from the threat of the people on the mountain road? This was hard to believe. Yet there seemed to be no other reasonable explanation. I tried to shine my torch through the thin plastic of the tent wall on to the creature apparently lurking nearby – but the task was hopeless. So I simply crouched down and listened. Her relaxed breathing continued. After a while I felt that the two of us had formed some undefined, unspoken bond. As if, together, we were less vulnerable to any passing intruder.

Suddenly more voices were audible. Some way off, but coming closer. At least two men were walking along the path towards the clearing. I could not see any light moving; they appeared not to have a torch. I dared not shine my torch for fear of giving away my position. On the other hand, the night was so dark it seemed likely the strangers would fail to see the tents and would trip over the guy ropes holding our fragile shelters upright. The voices grew louder still, and I knew I had to do something. I thought of running – but that seemed like a kind of suicide. What if the men were armed? And how would the beast react? Neither of us had moved. Then, when the voices were almost upon us and we were nearly certain to be discovered, I heard a rasping warning from the leopardess – an unmistakable snarl, only inches away from my left side. The talking stopped like a switch being flicked off, and a second or so later came the sound of footsteps running back along the path. There was no further communication from the leopardess. For the rest of the night, I lay motionless on my ground-sheet listening to the unhurried breathing of my strange companion against the eerie noises of the night.

In fact, I must have slept a bit, because when I awoke there were shreds of daylight heralding dawn, straggling through the upper branches of the forest. The front flap of my tent was still open. I was too frightened to move, but at long last, as the morning became lighter, and the greeting calls of the jungle birds became bolder, I plucked up the courage to peer out of my tent towards the spot where my night-time companion must have lain. Needless to say, she had gone. There was nothing to be seen – not even a scratch in the dust or a claw mark on the small anthill that had been her uneven resting place. The leopardess had vanished as silently as she had come.

A few minutes later, a concerned Thad Petersen called across our clearing: 'Are you all right, Chris?' 'Yes', I called back. 'Did you hear the commotion on the road?' 'Of course,' he replied, 'but they seem to have gone now.' Indeed, there was no one else around. I suppose the rebel exodus across the border took place at night to escape detection. 'I think it's fairly safe now', he added.

I went over to his tent. 'Did you see the leopard?' I asked. 'What leopard?' Thad inquired. 'Oh. I thought I saw her last night some time before midnight, after the commotion started. But I may have been mistaken.' My intimate feline encounter would have been too difficult to explain. And perhaps even more difficult to believe. So I never mentioned it to Thad, or to anyone else.

THE RIDDLE OF LEWA DOWNS

*Then the Ethiopian put his five fingers close together
. . . and pressed them all over the Leopard, and
wherever the five fingers touched they left five little
black marks, all close together. You can see them
on any Leopard's skin you like, Best Beloved.
Sometimes the fingers slipped and the marks got a
little blurred; but if you look closely at any
Leopard now you will see that there are always five
spots . . .*

Rudyard Kipling
'How the Leopard Got Its Spots',
Just-So Stories, 1902

A BLACK LEOPARD is one of the rarest animals in the world,
and one of the most difficult to see in the wild. It arises from an
abnormal development of the dark pigment melanin, resulting in
the animal's coat being very dark or black. But despite its unusual
darkness, the spots of the leopard can still be seen faintly on the coat,
especially in bright sunlight. Melanism is hereditary, but it is not
necessarily passed from one generation to the next, so that melanistic
individuals occur in mixed litters.

It is widely believed that the black leopard is more vicious than its
tawny counterpart, which might be due to the level of its acceptance
in the litter, if a single black leopard cub has to fight harder for its
place among its siblings. In medieval times the creature was said to
be friendly towards all animals except the dragon, which it lured

to its fate by exuding a particularly sweet odour. Later it was a symbol of Christ, until its savage nature became more widely known. Then the black leopard became a symbol of evil and hypocritical flattery.

Of course there are reports of black leopards being seen, and shot, in the jungles of southern India, particularly in the Kerala region and also in the Sinharaja rainforest of Sri Lanka. In 1959, the south Indian writer and hunter Kenneth Anderson published a collection of jungle stories entitled *The Black Panther of Sivanipalli*. Naturally, I have always wanted to see a black leopard for myself. Once I received a telephone call from Kerala informing me that local herdsmen had trapped such a black beast, known locally as 'the goat killer', in a deep pit. However, the animal died before I could get there.

Then, in 1999, Nigel Winser of the Royal Geographical Society told me of the sighting of a black leopard on Lewa Downs in the northern foothills of Mount Kenya. The Lewa Ranch – 40,000 acres of private land owned by the Craig family – is an enormous conservation area designed to protect elephants and other African game from poaching and human encroachment. The nearest town is Isiolo, beyond which is the vast and rugged expanse of northern Kenya that reaches right up to the Ethiopian border. Much of Lewa Downs is more than 6,500 feet in elevation, interspersed with deep river valleys and enormous outcroppings of rock.

Although I wanted to drop everything to go to Lewa, I was involved in a film project in Sri Lanka, which required two gruelling weeks filming around the island's ruined cities and in the Yala Game Reserve. The moment I returned to England, I immediately made plans to fly to Kenya to stay with the Craig family. In the meantime William Craig had arranged for a trio of game trackers to do some preparatory work, looking for any signs of the black leopard, such as pug marks or a kill, in an area of more than nine square miles around where it had been sighted.

I flew out of Heathrow airport on the night of 8 December, arrived in Nairobi early the following day, and transferred to a small six-seater Cessna plane that got me to Lewa in time for lunch. My three trackers, Mungai, Rikita and Alfred, were happy to see me but had no news of the leopard. Mungai, a member of the Kikuyu tribe, was dressed in ordinary safari fatigues, but Rikita and Alfred, both Maasai, wore their faded red cotton *olgaresha* cloaks slung over their shoulders. They were muscular, lean and beautiful, with long ochre-stained hair carefully braided and gathered together, tied in a bunch and draped down their backs.

The trackers were enthusiastic about the search, but not at all confident of success. Leopards are secretive, elusive and difficult to see at the best of times, but in December, after the 'short rains', with the area much greener than usual, the task would be almost impossible, they feared.

Exhausted and jet-lagged, I decided to have a quick sleep. The next thing I knew, Mungai was awakening me at five in the afternoon. I showered, had a cup of strong Kenyan coffee, got my camera equipment together and set off for a reconnaissance in the long-wheelbase Land Rover that was to be mine for the next eight days. The temperature was surprisingly cool for the equator, because of the altitude.

We coursed out away from the lodge towards the Lewa River, making our way through the marshes and yellow fever trees, and back around the far side of Cave Hill towards the Ngare Ndare forest. The circuit was about eighteen miles on the rough Lewa Downs roads. We saw herds of elephant, the rare Grevy's zebra, an occasional group of reticulated giraffe, a few white rhinoceros and one small herd of eland, but no cats – no lions, no cheetahs and definitely no sign of a leopard.

Night falls quickly in Africa and soon after six o'clock it was too dark to see, so we returned to the ranch, planning to start again before dawn the next day. To be back in the scrub forests of East Africa was a wonderful feeling.

Mungai woke me the following morning at five out of a very deep sleep. Outdoors it was still very dark, and very cold. I was shivering when I hauled myself out of bed and put on my safari clothes. Making my way by flashlight through the scrub to the courtyard of the Lewa Ranch, I found Rikita and Alfred waiting in the back of the Land Rover. I piled in beside Mungai, who did the driving.

The morning wind howled around us in the open vehicle. Mungai crouched over the steering wheel and peered into the darkness. A hyena furtively crossed in front of us, eyes shining in our headlights. Occasionally we saw zebra moving towards the river. There was as yet no sign of sunrise, but we could see from the stars that the sky was cloudless.

Within half an hour we were crossing the plains at the foot of Cave Hill, and minutes later the morning light stretched across the eastern sky. Only the Land Rover's engine disturbed the African morning. And then, as the sun's golden ball crept over the horizon, faintly out-lining Mount Kenya in the distance, came the morning chorus. Three crowned cranes perched high on a spreading umbrella acacia; an African tawny eagle made its high-pitched screech; a boubou emitted its plaintive call; and two ostriches strutted along the river road in front of us, oblivious of our mission. The bush was coming to life. I suppose my Maasai companions were entirely used to early morn-ings like this, but to me they are always spellbinding.

An hour later we stopped for coffee, when quite suddenly we heard an alarm call from an impala, and then the deep guttural sawing of a predator. 'Leopard', guessed Mungai, listening with one ear cocked towards the caves above the plain. The sound came again. We waited for a few minutes, heard nothing more and drove on.

I was certain we had heard a leopard and my two Maasai trackers agreed, particularly Rikita. But of course it was impossible to know what kind of leopard. I was certain the sound had come from high up on Cave Hill. We returned to the spot from where we first heard it, and listened again. Still nothing. 'Listen', I said. 'If there is a chance it was the black leopard, we must surround the hill and hope that he shows himself. We have to gamble.'

I suggested that Rikita wait secluded and hidden in the long brown grass at the foot of Cave Hill, and that Alfred sit higher up on the western rim of the hill. The Maasai, as I later learned, have incredible patience. The sun was high in the sky now, and I was asking them to expose themselves in the hot African sun for the greater part of the day. I gave my binoculars to Rikita, and the two Maasai youths silently slipped out of the Land Rover and across the plain to their lookout positions. These were about half a mile from where Mungai and I stationed ourselves on a hillock overlooking the entire south face of Cave Hill.

It was still only eight o'clock, and we prepared ourselves for a long, dry day. Mungai, who has astonishing vision, never took his eyes off the face of the hill. Because I had given my binoculars to Rikita I was forced to use my 400mm telephoto lens to range the hill from left to right, west to east. I was sure the best chance of seeing the black leopard was against the brown dried grass. We didn't say much, realizing that the plan was probably a futile one. But I was still hopeful.

It was tiring to look for a black dot on a brown hillside, especially after five hours of looking. Then I saw another Land Rover coursing its way across the river towards our hillock. At first I cursed it for disturbing our vigil, but soon realized it was Will Craig bringing us much-needed supplies of water and food. Will, although admiring our stamina, made no bones about the hopelessness of our quest.

An hour after Will's departure Rikita reappeared on our hillock. He held out his hand and showed us a single black hair. It could have been from any animal, and I suggested a zebra. But Rikita said this was impossible; zebras are far too lazy to climb up Cave Hill. He was convinced that it was the hair of a leopard and that we should continue our watch.

Three hours later we were still there. It was four o'clock and the heat of the day was ebbing a little. Rikita appeared again on the rise below us, hurrying. He spoke quickly to Mungai in Swahili and pointed to the back of Cave Hill. He claimed he had seen something moving in the long grass and that it might be a leopard. He wasn't sure, but if it were a leopard then it might take advantage of the coolness to move out of the shade and protection of the grass to a higher position on the hill. Mungai continued to scan the face of the hill. He was motionless, his eyes trained towards the eastern base of Cave Hill, towards the river, above the long dry brown grass of the plains.

Suddenly he spoke quietly to me: 'Quick, quick. There, the leopard, moving. Get your camera. Take the glasses. Look – above the acacia tree – to the left. Do you see it? You'll have to wait. I'll tell you when it moves. There. Now.'

And then I saw it, just as Rikita had said, an indistinct black shape moving slowly across the face of Cave Hill. Up the hill diagonally, and then out of sight again behind long grass.

'OK', said Mungai to Rikita. 'You stay with Christopher; I'll go and get Alfred. Don't lose sight of the leopard. It's getting dark, so you'll have to keep your eyes on him.'

And then Mungai drove off, returning with an exhausted, parched Alfred a few minutes later. Rikita hadn't taken his eyes off the place where the leopard was crouching. Neither had I. And then we all saw the leopard again, looking at us across the divide between our hillock and Cave Hill. He lifted his black head above the grass and then lowered it again. Cautious – even furtive. A typical tawny leopard would have been quite invisible among the light brown tones of the scorched hill grass. But this was a black leopard – a rare privilege for us. We watched the cat for almost ten minutes, but there was not enough light to take any decent photographs. And then the sky became dimmer still, and it was almost evening. Another, night-time, African world was stirring.

We had no proof that we had seen the leopard. Although Will Craig believed us, we knew we needed to get good photographs. So at five o'clock the next morning Mungai woke me once again. But this time he had brought with him a Maasai elder, and old man called Taraiyo from the Ilng'uesi reserve, who worked for the Craig family on the Lewa Ranch. Mungai told me that Taraiyo wanted to talk to me and also wanted to come with us that day to search for the leopard. I agreed.

While I was gathering myself together, drinking strong coffee, packing my cameras, Taraiyo asked me over and over again, did you see the leopard? A black leopard? Are you sure? Is Mungai sure? I told him I was, but the news seemed to upset Taraiyo. He grew silent and thoughtful as we piled our gear into the Land Rover. He squeezed in the back with Rikita and Alfred. As we made our way in the darkness to the foot of Cave Hill Taraiyo leant over my shoulder and said: 'If you saw the black leopard yesterday that is bad.' I looked around at him. He was serious.

'Why?' I asked. Taraiyo didn't answer. Rikita and Alfred remained silent. Twenty minutes later we crossed the river and wound our way across the plains to the foot of Cave Hill. It was still dark, but I got my cameras ready, as well as my video camera-recorder, and put them on the dashboard. We waited in silence for the dawn, Mungai and I sitting, the three Maasai standing in the back of the Land Rover.

Suddenly both Rikita and Alfred shouted: 'Chui. There's the leopard!'

'Where?' I cried, standing up suddenly and grabbing the video camera. I looked out on to Cave Hill. 'No, not there – there', Rikita yelled excitedly. And there on a small plain not fifty yards from the Land Rover, towards the base of Cave Hill, was the melanistic cat. I pressed the Sony camera into action, with fully extended telephoto lens, and kept filming while Mungai started the engine and drove very slowly towards the large, obviously male, black leopard. We guessed he had been down to the river to quench his thirst, but now he had seen us and scurried away, yet not far. I kept filming whether or not the leopard was in the frame. He kept moving. No one said anything. And then we lost him. I must have got about three minutes of the animal on film.

Taraiyo, who had been completely silent for some time, said: 'Up there in the caves.' We looked up the hill and saw the leopard again, and I got perhaps another minute of the beast on film, further away but still clearly visible. It was lighter now, and the leopard made its way up the side of the escarpment, up the hill towards the caves where he obviously planned to spend the day out of the glaring sun.

I replayed the footage. It was all there. Some of it was poor and very shaky, particularly what I had shot while the Land Rover was moving. But the leopard was definitely there, thank God. In the excitement I had completely forgotten to take any still photographs.

'What do you want to do now?' Mungai asked.

With increasing heat we knew the leopard would not show himself again until the late afternoon. There was a chance he would venture onto the plains to hunt, but this would not happen until much later. So we decided to go back to the ranch for breakfast.

None of the others had ever seen a black leopard before, not even Taraiyo, who was about seventy years old. But he did not seem particularly happy. I was sure that he knew something that he wasn't telling me. So I arranged to meet him later in the morning. But first I wanted to show the footage of the black leopard to Will Craig. He watched it with speechless amazement.

I talked to Taraiyo in a room next to the Lewa stables. I did not think that I could broach the subject of the black leopard straight away, so I decided to try to learn from him something of the Maasai, their traditions and ways. He spoke English haltingly, searching for the right words, but he understood much more than he could speak. He clearly had a keen sense of history and a proud knowledge of legend and ritual. He was also incredibly superstitious.

The Maasai are the most pastoral people of Africa and have not until very recently had laws on agricultural land. They speak the Maa language and seem always to have been divided into two groups. There are the agricultural Maasai such as the Wa-Arusha (of northern Tanzania) and the Baraguyu. And then there are the Maasai of north-eastern Kenya, for example the Ilng'uesi, Taraiyo's tribe. Although the Ilng'uesi do practise agriculture, they prefer a pastoral life, keeping cattle and moving across the plains between grazing lands with the change in the seasons.

The pre-colonial history of the Maasai is shrouded in myth. It is believed that they originated in a crater-like country – almost certainly the north-western shore of Lake Rudolph (now Lake Turkana) in northern Kenya) – surrounded by steep escarpments, which some of them left as a result of a prolonged period of drought. These Maasai moved to the highlands of Kenya, where they live to this day. The advent of British colonialism put a check on their further southward expansion, but not before the Maasai had reached the northern region of what was then Tanganyika. Highways for commerce with Buganda were important to the British, for Buganda gave access to the River Nile and ultimately the Suez Canal, a gateway to the economic wealth of India and the East. These highways lay through Maasai land.

Taraiyo seemed to welcome my understanding of Maasai history. He agreed that Maasai power and wealth had been reduced with the arrival of Europeans in Africa. But, he said, despite the pressure on the Maasai to curtail their pastoral activities, the tribe retained its beliefs and traditions.

'We are not really Africans', Taraiyo continued. 'We come from the Nile near the lands that used to be called Abyssinia and which is now called Ethiopia. We were not meant to stay in one place like now, growing vegetables and digging the earth. We are warriors and herdsmen. We are what you call nomads, following the rain and the new grass to feed our herds. This is important to us. This is our wealth. We kill anyone who stops our freedom. But now there are new laws. We cannot move from one area to another. We must go where we are told to go, even though this is our land. They have taken away our land and taken away our freedom. And now they teach us the white man's way in the schools where we have to send our children. If you stop our freedom we will die. We cannot be prisoners and we cannot use our hands for labour work. We are warriors . . .'

There was a pause and I decided to risk all and ask him the question I'd been dying to ask. 'But what about the black leopard? Why are you so worried that we have seen one of the rarest animals in the world? This is a very lucky thing for us.'

'No. No. No', Taraiyo replied in quite an agitated state. There was a pained look in his eyes. 'It is not a lucky thing. It is very unlucky and very bad. Always there are problems for us. First there are good rains and then more children, but always after that there will be no rain and drought and bad times. This is always the way when we see the panther, what you call the black leopard. It is evil and should be killed. If you do not kill it and use the oil from the body to rub on the children, then they will be sick. Always this is the way. We must pray to Maa. He is the God that sees these things. He is looking now. We must give the black animal to him. God does not eat mankind. Evil cannot be contained. Darkness has ears, and you will soon understand that he who has a sharp mouth conquers the world.'

I said nothing for a while. Taraiyo looked at his feet as if embarrassed by what he had said, as if he had spoken of something that should not be mentioned to an outsider. These beliefs, he seemed to say, should only be discussed among the elders. He seemed uneasy. Although I invited Taraiyo to come with us that afternoon, I was not surprised that he declined, saying he must return to Ilng'uesi and his people, as there was no more work for him at Lewa Ranch. We slowly walked out into the African sunlight together, but then we went our separate ways.

'Where shall we go?' Mungai asked me as Rikita, Alfred and I climbed into the old Land Rover later that afternoon. 'To the plains between the river and Cave Hill', I replied without much hesitation. 'Do you think it's too early?' It was only half past three and the sun was high in the sky. It was far too hot for predators to start out on their evening activities. 'It'll take us about half an hour to get there', Mungai replied. 'If the leopard wants to hunt he'll have to come down to the plains before it gets dark.'

And so we made our way out, away from the ranch, through the scrub jungle, across the Lewa River, and into the long dried-grass plains below Cave Hill. At the foot of Cave Hill a lone thorn acacia was obscuring part of our view of the hill face, and I thought of asking Mungai to move the Land Rover further along the track to the base of the hill. But it was still too hot, so I simply focused on the hill and a shallow ditch at the foot of it. There was no sign of the leopard.

And then I looked over and into the branches of the acacia tree and saw a very slight movement in a stick hanging down from the shadows under the tree about ten or twelve feet above the ground. What was it? Probably only a branch moving in the wind, but I kept my eyes on it. And then it moved again. Could it possibly be the leopard's tail? The tree was certainly an ideal platform for a leopard to prospect its territory.

'Mungai,' I said, 'take these glasses and have a look. Don't move. Don't anybody move.' We were all sitting down. 'Look just to the right of the main trunk of the tree, on the right-hand branch. Can you see something hanging down? What do you think?'

'I can't see definitely', Mungai replied. 'We're too far away. Keep your small camera focused on the branch and I'll move the Land Rover closer.'

'Don't move or stand up', I said. 'Go towards the tree, very slowly, really slowly. Not too far. Maybe about twenty or thirty yards.' And as we moved closer, the shadows above the low branches of the acacia grew a little less dark. 'Stop', I said. 'Give me the glasses.' And then my heart leapt. For there, on the low right-hand branch, with its black tail hanging down, was the black leopard. It was looking straight at us.

We had switched off the engine. I focused the video camera directly on the creature, which was still quite far away. I filmed the leopard looking at us from the shadows of the branching acacia for about a minute, but then he got up onto the branches. 'Damn, we've disturbed him. We've come too close', I said. I still had my camera on the leopard, as he slowly crept down the jutting limbs of the tree and silently leapt off the branch into the long brown grass below. We sat motionless for about five minutes, and then I said: 'Mungai. Drive up to the tree slowly. Maybe he's on the ground in the grass and we'll see him move towards the hill.'

Very slowly we went forward until we were almost under the tree. But still we saw nothing. And then I did something stupid and dangerous. Desperate to get more footage, I got out of the Land Rover, slid myself into the long grass and walked slowly towards the tree. I told Mungai to stay with the vehicle, and told Alfred and Rikita to fan out either side of the tree about twenty yards away from where we had last seen the leopard. I kept my camera on in case something moved, not really caring what a cornered leopard might do. Reaching the base of the tree without seeing anything, I waited patiently. Surely he must be here. I looked back. Mungai was glancing at us anxiously. Then I quietly told Alfred to move towards Rikita on the other side of the tree. 'Just move slowly', I said. Alfred moved. He had taken only about four steps when he pointed in front of him and said: 'The leopard is here. He is going to go up the hill.'

I couldn't see anything but I moved quickly forward, the camera still filming, trained in the direction in which Alfred was pointing. He was standing still. And then I saw the leopard again, moving slowly, picking his way up the bank at the base of Cave Hill, between the low scrub bushes, with careful grace, his long black tail behind him, his large black head low to the ground. The sun was darting on his shiny black back, allowing us to see the faint rosettes on his body as he moved purposefully away from us. I kept the camera on, never once looking up. And then in less than thirty seconds it was all over. The leopard disappeared into some thick grass further up the hill, towards the escarpment below the caves. I turned my camera off, looked towards Alfred and Rikita, and smiled. When I looked down at my boots and trousers I saw that my feet were covered in ticks.

No one ever saw the black leopard again.

I left Kenya after a week at Lewa Downs with the dire warnings of Taraiyo still occupying my thoughts. As he had predicted, there were very bad times in the area for almost an entire year, with unusually low rainfall and swarms of locusts. With no work in Lewa, Taraiyo remained at Ilng'uesi. Now, ten years later, I find myself wondering what has become of him, and whether the story of his once-in-a-lifetime sighting of the black leopard will be passed down to the children of this small but proud warrior community.

KILIMANJARO:
HEMINGWAY IN AFRICA

*Kilimanjaro is a snow covered mountain 19,710 feet
high, and is said to be the highest mountain in
Africa. Its western summit is called 'Nguja Ngai',
the House of God. Close to the western summit
there is the dried and frozen carcass of a leopard.
No one has explained what the leopard was
seeking at that altitude.*

Ernest Hemingway,
'The Snows of Kilimanjaro', 1936

EVER SINCE I first went to Africa in the 1980s in search of the source
of the River Nile, geography, wildlife, history, tribal lore, legend and
literature have lured me to Mount Kilimanjaro, the highest mountain
in the entire continent. Located in northern Tanzania near the border
with Kenya, its base is about thirty miles from east to west and about
eighteen miles from north to south. Its snowy peak, Kibo, at 19,340
feet, was probably observed two millennia ago by ancient Greek
sailors who reached the East African coast. But the first European
known to have seen the mountain for certain was the Reverend Ernst
Rebmann, in 1849. He sent home reports, which 'excited such angry
and unseemly contests amongst our usually sedate though speculative
carpet-geographers in England as rendered a further inspection
highly necessary', wrote John Hanning Speke in the 1850s at the time
of his search for the source of the Nile. Speke's fellow explorer – and

one of my heroes – Richard Burton, 'desirous of having a peep at the snowy Kilimanjaro Mountain', made the rugged journey there, followed by other European travellers over the next few decades. But the first European to climb to the summit was Hans Meyer in 1889.

Kilimanjaro is a volcano (in fact, three volcanoes, Mawenzi, Kibo and Shira), which is theoretically dormant, not extinct, not far from the volcanically formed East African Rift Valley. It has not erupted since pre-human times, although it did show a small amount of volcanic activity just over two hundred years ago, and sulphurous gases can still be smelt in particular areas of the mountain near the summit crater. However, volcanic fire has nothing to do with the mountain's name. According to Monsignor Alexandre Le Roy, who described his 1880s journey to Kilimanjaro from Zanzibar in his book *Au Kilima-Ndjaro (Afrique orientale)*, *kilima* was a common word in many of the region's languages, including Swahili, for 'mountain'. But he had trouble finding out what *ndjaro* meant. Some local people told him that it meant 'big'; others that it meant 'whiteness' – obviously because of the mountain's snow cap; still others that it derived from a Maasai word meaning 'water', because of the many streams that flowed from the mountain.

Before the European colonization of Africa, there were more than a hundred sovereign Chagga tribal chieftains on the lower slopes of Kilimanjaro, notably Orombo of the Keni region, Sina of Kibosho, Rindi of Moshi, Marealle of Marangu and Abdiel Shangali of Machame. By 1899, violent clashes had reduced this number to thirty-seven chieftaincies. When the slave and ivory trade was at its height in the mid-nineteenth century, Kilimanjaro was a meeting place for caravans using the route across Maasailand from the coast to Victoria Nyanza. Coastal traders bought ivory from the Chagga rulers and obtained provisions from the Chagga markets. Chagga rulers provided safe campsites for the caravans and safe passage through their territory.

Colonization by the Germans between 1886 and 1916 brought rapid and far-reaching change to the world of the Chagga, introducing them to cash, Christianity, formal education and the commercial cultivation of coffee. A cash-based economy came to replace the barter economy whose monetary units had been cattle, pigs and iron hoes.

The British controlled Kilimanjaro from 1916 to 1961. The first British administrator of the area, Sir Charles Dundas, came to be admired by the Chagga for his efforts to promote the interests of native coffee growers in the face of colonial plantation owners' objections. Many Chagga had grown coffee in their own gardens for their personal use, but Dundas established the Kilimanjaro Native Planters Association, which protected the commercial rights of native growers. During their tenure in power, the British oversaw many political changes: in 1928 a Council of Chiefs representing the three major groupings of chieftaincies was introduced, and in 1960 the district's first president was elected. After Tanganyika became independent in 1961 and joined with Zanzibar to become Tanzania, the Kilimanjaro region became a collection of seventeen municipal districts whose capital is Moshi, a former chieftaincy. It continued to be important, not least because it supplied the country with a disproportionate number of administrators and business leaders.

At a religious level, Kilimanjaro has had a mystical significance to man ever since he first set eyes on it. The Maasai people view the mountain as holy, and the Chagga who live on its slopes believe its heights to be the home of the sun god Ruwa, the great protector and provider who created nature, man and beasts. When they wish to pray to Ruwa, the Chagga face the mountain; and their dead are buried with heads pointing towards it. The mountain's flat summit known as Kibo is particularly revered by the Chagga, because it is thought to bring rain. Its western summit, Mawenzi, 'is called "Nguja Ngai," the House of God', wrote Ernest Hemingway in 'The Snows of Kilimanjaro', his most celebrated story about Africa.

Immediately after this Hemingway adds – most intriguingly to me: 'Close to the western summit there is the dried and frozen carcass of a leopard. No one has explained what the leopard was seeking at that altitude.' Leopards are the most dangerous, secretive and alluring of all the African cats. Perhaps it is their combination of indolent beauty and deadly cunning that attracts many of us so strongly. Or possibly it is their solitariness, for leopards are anti-social creatures, seen together only during the mating season, and unlike lions they hunt alone and almost exclusively at night. For anyone who likes a personal challenge, trying to catch a glimpse of this unique creature is as irresistible as the sirens' song. No wonder Hemingway made a leopard into a tantalizing artistic symbol in this story.

The leopard carcass he mentions was no fiction. It was found in 1926 by an English mountaineer, Donald Latham, during his climb to the summit. Latham published photographs of the carcass on a pile of rocks and of a bearer proudly holding it above his head. In his description of the ascent he explains: 'A remarkable discovery was the remains of a leopard, sun-dried and frozen, right at the crater rim. The beast must have wandered there and died of exposure.' Latham thought that the leopard had been hunting, had lost its way in a blizzard, and had been driven up the mountain to escape the cold. Hemingway, however, offers no explanation. Rather, he sets up the presence of the leopard near the summit in the prologue to his story as a riddle that the reader must try to answer through the tale that follows.

In 'The Snows of Kilimanjaro' Harry, a writer on safari, is dying in the shadow of the great peak. Waiting at the base of the mountain for the plane that is his only hope of rescue, he dwells on his past and the mistakes he has made. Through his sniping at his wife and his recollections of Europe, the reader learns of Harry's marriage to a rich woman he does not love, of the gangrenous leg that is going to kill him, and of his intense wartime and post-war experiences that will now never see print because Harry has betrayed his writing talent for a life of luxury.

Although Kilimanjaro broods over Hemingway's story, the leopard is mentioned only once. Still, its image haunted me, along with many of the story's other images. 'The Snows of Kilimanjaro', and its origins in Hemingway's life, seemed worthy of fresh investigation. Together with Karen Blixen's *Out of Africa* and Beryl Markham's *West with the Night*, Hemingway's story is at the centre of an extensive collection of books, maps, photographs and articles about East Africa that I have accumulated while travelling there in search of wildlife and the sources of the Nile. Although the story is brief compared to Hemingway's novels, it is perfect. It encapsulates the enduring themes of the Hemingway opus: how a man can be heroic in the face of danger, war, slaughter and death; how he can remain true to a personal vision when everyday life conspires to cloud it; and how a writer's life must inspire his writings. For as the Hemingway scholar Jeffrey Meyers writes in *Hemingway: Life into Art*, 'One of Hemingway's fundamental aesthetic principles was that fiction must be based on actual experience.' Why is Hemingway's most penetrating look at a writer's failure set in Africa? What exactly was Hemingway's relationship with Africa? What was he seeking there?

Theodore Roosevelt was Hemingway's childhood idol. The young Ernest – his interest in Africa sparked by Carl Akeley's collection of stuffed African animals on display in Chicago – devoured the numerous magazine articles describing Roosevelt's African safari of 1909. Roosevelt's books, *African Game Trails* (1910) and *Through the Brazilian Wilderness* (1914), had an honoured place on Hemingway's shelves next to Akeley's memoir, *In Brightest Africa* (1923). Roosevelt inspired Hemingway to such an extent that, aged sixteen, he was quite certain he wanted to be a pioneer or an explorer of one of the last great frontiers – Africa, South America or the Arctic.

In 1921 Hemingway had his first encounter with fiction about Africa. He was fascinated by *Batouala*, a newly published first novel by an unknown black French writer, René Maran, which had just won the Goncourt Prize. *Batouala* was the subject of Hemingway's inaugural professional book review, published in the *Toronto Star*. It is significant not only for being a first for him, but also because it hints at the qualities we now associate with Hemingway's own fiction. At this early stage, Hemingway had yet to establish his own style, and the myth of 'Papa' Hemingway was a long way off, yet his review of *Batouala* shows the excitement of its writer's imagination stimulated by a novelist's convincing picture of an unfamiliar, enticing African world.

Despite the persistence of Hemingway mania today, Hemingway in Africa is a subject relatively neglected both by the reading public and by scholars. His two African short stories, 'The Snows of Kilimanjaro' and 'The Short Happy Life of Francis Macomber', both published in 1936, are rightly judged to be among his best work, but his non-fiction book *Green Hills of Africa*, which recounts his first safari in 1933–34, remains underrated, and the posthumously published *True at First Light*, about his second safari in 1953–54, is widely dismissed as the ramblings of an ageing and ailing man capable only of flashes of his former brilliance. Moreover, few seem to realize that embedded within another posthumously published work, *The Garden of Eden*, is an emotional short story of an African elephant hunt. Its inclusion within an experimental book shows that Hemingway never got Africa out of his system. For him, Africa was a readily available metaphor for escape, as well as something much more. Through all the adventures, travels, romances and achievements of Hemingway's early career, Africa remained a constant dream. He fell in love with the *idea* of Africa in his teens long before he fell in love with the real Africa. When, at thirty-four, he finally made the journey to Kenya and Tanganyika, he was bewitched by its exotic landscape. He longed to return almost before he had left. Twenty years would pass before he did, and that second safari came close to killing him; nevertheless, he said it was one of the happiest times in his life.

In *True at First Light*, Hemingway writes: 'Something, or something awful or something wonderful was certain to happen on every day in this part of Africa. Every morning when you woke it was as exciting as though you were going to compete in a downhill ski race or drive a bobsled on a fast run. Something, you knew, would happen and usually before eleven o'clock. I never knew of a morning in Africa when I woke that I was not happy.'

I decided to visit Hemingway country in Kenya, Tanzania (Tanganyika in Hemingway's time) and Uganda, and write a book, *Hemingway in Africa*. By following in his footsteps and experiencing at first hand the places he wrote about on his two safaris, I sensed that one could understand Hemingway's attraction to Africa in a deeper way than his many biographers had, excellent though their books are about his life in America and Europe. Of course, I knew it would be impossible to consider Hemingway's Africa separate from colonial issues. The Africas of the great Victorian explorers like Speke and Burton, of Akeley and Roosevelt, of Maran, Blixen and Markham, of Hemingway's first safari in 1933 and his second in 1953, and the Africa of my own safaris are each different, as they come nearer to our own time, farther away from the tribal kingdoms and natural wilderness of Africa that met the eyes of David Livingstone. Yet something of the original Africa, and of colonial Africa before it went irreparably wrong, did remain, in my experience. This was the Africa that Hemingway sought. And this was what I too went after. On my last African safari, I would stop where Hemingway stopped and look where he looked, in a quest for a convincing explanation of his strange and profound affection for Africa. At the heart of it, I knew, lay Kilimanjaro.

Surprisingly, and maybe significantly in the light of his story, Hemingway never climbed the mountain. But I hoped to do so. One of the biggest disappointments in my life was the slow and reluctant realization that I had left this particular expedition too late. My right hip and shoulder had long been riddled with arthritis and it would have been foolish to undertake the long climb, which lasts up to a week there and back. Even so, when I reached Kenya, I was still hoping I might conquer my arthritis and manage the trek. One of the first things I did after landing at Mombasa was to visit a faith healer.

I have a longstanding interest – not strong enough to call a belief – in the arcane practices of faith healers in Africa and Asia. This particular healer lived off the beaten track in the village of Kathilani, near Machakos, not far from Nairobi, in an area that is the home of the Wakamba tribe – an important people for Hemingway, who tells of his romance with a Wakamba girl named Debba in *True at First Light*. The healer knew we were coming, but when we at last made it to his village he was in the middle of performing a rather painful-looking procedure on a young woman in front of a crowd of curious Wakamba. I was unsure what sickness was being expunged from the woman as she lay, stripped to the waist, on the hot red earth. The healer wore a white cloak, and during the course of the half-hour treatment, he dug his knife into her flesh and rubbed a dark powder into the wound. This strange powder was only the final stage: before administering it he had worked his way through a Thompson's gazelle horn, a warthog tusk, two emperor shells and a small calabash, and had even used a wildebeest whip. At length the woman got up, apparently unharmed, though it was impossible to tell if the treatment had been effective.

I decided to take the plunge. Through an interpreter, I told the healer where I suffered from arthritis. He agreed to perform a ritual treatment on me similar to the one we had just witnessed. The knife wounds pierced my skin, though not deeply, and they certainly hurt.

There was blood. After rubbing the dark powder into my wounds, he gave me half a tumbler of a pungent grey fluid to drink. It tasted like brewed garlic cloves – absolutely foul. And its effect was immediate. I sweated profusely and felt quite bilious on the journey back to the ranch house where I was staying, as our Land Rover juddered over steep paths to regain the tarred road. The whole venture was in fact a risky and rather stupid medical experiment, for which I was later scolded by a London doctor as he handed me a negative test report for HIV. But at the time I went under the healer's knife, apart from the hope of curing my arthritis, I also felt that the experience might help me in a small way to understand the relationship between the danger Hemingway willingly courted in his life and the vitality he expressed in his writing.

It was quite a journey following Hemingway from Machakos to Nairobi across the Tanzanian border to Arusha, and thence to Mto Wa Mbu (Mosquito Village) and up the escarpment where we could look down on Lake Manyara. Although our route coincided with Hemingway's in 1933–34, we did not have his option of hunting for the pot. From Lake Manyara we drove towards the dormant Oldeani volcano to camp in the Mongola district near Lake Eyasi and the Ngorongoro crater. Here the Hemingway party hunted for lions. We found the lush land still rich in game. Then we went south to Babati, near where the kudu hunt that is the narrative focus of *Green Hills of Africa* took place. Here we were sidetracked at a Hadza settlement and invited to join their primitive early morning hunt: the Africa of yesteryear trying to survive in the Africa of today.

Since Hemingway was fascinated by fear all his life, the question of a man's bravery in the face of danger was a natural topic of conversation on his first safari. The circumstances of a hunter's losing his nerve would likely have been campfire talk between Hemingway and his hunter-guide Philip Percival as they swigged companionable aperitifs after a long day in the field. He also used a real-life incident in 'The Short Happy Life of Francis Macomber', based on Colonel J. H. Patterson, the ruthless railway engineer who had earlier killed the man-eating lions of Tsavo. Patterson acted as hunter-guide for the Hon. Audley Blyth and his wife on safari, but returned from the bush with only Mrs Blyth, whom he later married. How her husband died is still shrouded in mystery.

Driving south from Babati we approached two more camps used by Hemingway near Kolo and Kondoa, from where he hunted kudu, buffalo, Thompson's gazelle and rhinoceros. After Kondoa, we took a sharp turn to the east across the Maasai steppe through wide-open hunting country alive with game to Kibaya, Kiberashi and Handeni, a further Hemingway campsite.

Handeni was now a sleepy, dirty town. Hemingway would not have believed how much seventy years had altered his original tiny settlement. East of Handeni the *miombo* was being cleared for small settlements. We drove further out, away from Western influence, going north-east towards Korogwe until we once more saw Maasai *morani* in their red cloaks and thatched huts, and in the distance the cloud-enveloped Usambara Mountains. This was where Hemingway returned after a convalescence from amoebic dysentery in Nairobi and vigorously embarked on his quest to bag a live kudu, but his run of bad luck continued. On his penultimate day there, he shot two beautiful kudu bulls – only to find that his friend Charles Thompson had gone one better, bagging (in Hemingway's words) 'the biggest, widest, darkest, longest-curling, heaviest, most unbelievable pair of kudu horns in the world'. An envious Hemingway said that he never wanted to see his own bulls' horns again.

With their last trophies taken and the February rains falling hard, the Hemingway party left the bush for Tanga and Malindi on the Kenyan coast. We followed in their tracks. Fishing in Malindi, Hemingway was now fully in his element. Inevitably, I had to visit the hotel at Watamu from which he is said to have fished. But Gary

Cullen, the manager of the hotel, originally called Seafarers and now re-named Hemingways, told me that Hemingway had never actually fished out of Watamu; he only drank at its bar. Surprisingly, given the hotel's name-change, Cullen said he had little time for the writer: 'If anyone was more successful than him, he became unbearable. Everyone wanted to treat him as a hero, but however hard they tried they eventually couldn't stand him.'

Hemingway left Kenya in 1934 with the firm intention of returning the following year. By the time he actually came back, two decades later, he was on to his fourth wife and had become an international celebrity, particularly after the publication of his novel *For Whom the Bell Tolls* in 1940. Some of his writings had been made into movies, including his two famous African stories, filmed as *The Macomber Affair* (1946) and *The Snows of Kilimanjaro* (1952). On his second safari, he was accompanied by Earl Theisen, a photographer from *Look* magazine, who was keen to shoot photographs of the great writer posing with impressive trophies.

Most of Hemingway's second safari, a complicated journey, was spent in the traditional lands of the Wakamba tribe. This is where Hemingway shot his first lion, the only animal he really wanted to bag. Then the Hemingway party struck camp and drove east into the Tsavo region to the new Fig Tree camp. On our way there through arid savannah I was jolted out of my day-dream of being on safari with Hemingway by the sight of a vast giraffe graveyard. In a land of predators and scavengers, death is never far away, but this field of bones was strangely affecting. It looked like the work of poachers. Pitching our camp in Tsavo was a chaotic experience. We had left it too late and had to struggle in the dark with tent poles while searching in vain for tent pegs and the usual safari paraphernalia amid criss-crossing torch beams and increasingly fractious shouts.

At Fig Tree camp, Theisen, restless for photos of Hemingway with his trophies, persuaded him to pose in front of a leopard shot by someone else. This famous photograph is therefore a classic of misleading Hemingway publicity. Even his wife Mary was moved to protest, but Hemingway retorted with bombast: 'I'll get a leopard to salve your conscience.' From Fig Tree camp the Hemingways went south to Tanganyika to meet his son Patrick, who had bought a farm in 1951 and was living there with his American wife. Then they returned to an earlier camp at Kimana. But with the coming of the rains the place had become uninhabitable and Hemingway soon left the camp, never again to go hunting in Africa, except in the imagined world of *True at First Light*, an abridgement made by his son of Hemingway's 'African Journal', which ran to more than two hundred thousand words by the time of his death in 1961.

Although the reader would never know it from *True at First Light*, Hemingway's second African expedition came to a highly dramatic close that nearly cost him his life, like his central character, the writer Harry, in 'The Snows of Kilimanjaro'. On 21 January 1954, the Hemingways took off in a light aircraft, stopping first at Bukavu on Lake Kivu and the next day flying north up the lake following the channel between Lake Edward and Lake George. An overnight stop at Entebbe was followed by more lake skimming, across the southern tip of Lake Albert, then over marshland along the Victoria Nile, until the party reached Murchison Falls – and disaster. Murchison Falls is not a vast cataract like Victoria Falls, but it is a very powerful rush of water (as I know from photographing it at length in my pursuit of the sources of the Nile). Danger lurks everywhere. As Mary Hemingway took photographs, the pilot Roy Marsh angled the aircraft to help his passenger get a better shot. Circling for the third time, Marsh swerved to avoid a flight of ibis and ripped into an abandoned, almost invisible, telegraph wire that sliced off the plane's rudder and radio antenna. It came down in trees three miles from the Falls. By an extraordinary stroke of luck, all three emerged relatively unscathed; Mary with cracked ribs, Ernest with heavy bruises on his shoulders and legs, and Marsh relatively unharmed. But with the nearest village forty-five miles away, their radio dead, and the rumble of dangerous animals nearby, they had little choice but to salvage the last of the whisky, move uphill and pitch camp.

Worse was to come. Rescue arrived the next day when a privately chartered boat took them to Butia. Another pilot, Reggie Cartwright, was now eager to fly the Hemingway party to Entebbe. On take-off the twelve-seater rose, then nose-dived and burst into flame. The metal door buckled in the heat but Cartwright, Marsh and Mary Hemingway were able to make their escape through a small window. Ernest Hemingway, however, was too large to get out this way. He worked frantically to force open the door, and eventually battered it open with his forehead. As a result of the accident, he suffered a damaged kidney and liver, head wounds, burns, a dislocated shoulder, and the temporary loss of hearing in one ear and vision in one eye. News of the crashes had already spread around the world and the plane's passengers were assumed to be dead. In Nairobi, the severely injured Hemingway enjoyed the rare honour of reading his own obituaries. Their near-universal praise may well have played a part in his receiving the Nobel Prize for literature the following year.

Like Hemingway, my safari ended with a plane flight. But instead of a near-fatal disaster, our finale was, thankfully, a minor miracle. I took a flight around Mount Kilimanjaro.

It was a dazzling dawn. We left Arusha airport at 6.45 a.m. Nearly thirty minutes later, we were approaching Kilimanjaro. On the right we saw the jagged peak of Mawenzi and on the left the stunning, square-topped peak of Kibo. As we flew directly into the blazing light the sun itself seemed suddenly to shift, shooting brilliant beams of light from the snow-capped heights, nearly 20,000 feet above sea level.

We circled the summit, past Leopard Point at the eastern edge of the crater, around past the north-eastern limits of Gilman's Point, then around the flat, raggedy slopes of Shira and back again to the south side. Higher this time, we made our second pass around the eastern edge and Leopard Point. The great peak that appeared on our left over the southern rim of the crater was Uhuru – the highest point in Africa. We made our third pass, green tents visible below us. Then Kibo hut. Again we flew between Mawenzi and Kibo and there once more was Leopard Point, poking up as a brown pinnacle from the eastern depths of the crater. For what seemed an eternal moment we were suspended over the centre of the crater, gazing directly into its depths.

I could see for myself why the Maasai call Kilimanjaro the House of God. I of course looked as closely as I could at Leopard Point, the place where Donald Latham had found the carcass in 1926 that had influenced Hemingway's story; where the leopard that had inspired me to follow Hemingway had wandered and died from cold. Now I could see for myself just how high the intrepid creature had climbed and how far removed it had been from its familiar terrain. What it was seeking at that altitude was no clearer to me than before. But why Hemingway had lit upon this specific image to open 'The Snows of Kilimanjaro' – why the leopard had resonated with him – did seem clarified.

For Hemingway, I think the leopard's upwards exploration came to stand for artistic endeavour, even though, artist that he was, he chose to leave the symbolism unspoken. In journeying away from familiar terrain, the leopard was set apart from all other leopards, and though it died alone, it was not forgotten; its preserved carcass on the mountain is testament to its journey. Consequently we remember this leopard, and it intrigues us and causes us to reflect.

Hemingway must have seen himself in the leopard's rarefied ascent. The true artist, driven by unknown forces, breaks away from routine and embarks on an exploration of the unfamiliar. In making this journey, his name is preserved. Hemingway's compulsion to write and to write well, his desire to achieve the sharpest observation and the most enduring prose, was certainly in part a bid to cheat death. As he said of literature, if it is good, 'many people remember you and they tell it to their children, and their children and grand-children remember... And if it's good enough, it will last as long as there are human beings.'

Hemingway does not suggest that the artist can reach the summit. Only that if he is serious about his art, he should attempt to get as near to it as he can. It is only when Harry, the dying writer in 'The Snows of Kilimanjaro', recognizes this truth, however painful, that he is rewarded with a vision of the mountain's peak. Dreaming that the rescue plane is carrying him away, Harry looks out of the window and 'there, ahead, all he could see, as wide as all the world, great, high, and unbelievably white in the sun, was the square top of Kilimanjaro. And then he knew that there was where he was going.'

The linking of artistic pursuit and the search for immortality is hardly a new concept. But Hemingway's African context allowed for a fresh development of the theme. Perhaps this is because Africa, above all other places he lived in, was like a crucible in which a new life could be formed. In Africa, absurdly beautiful landscape is an arena for terrifying natural forces. Mount Kilimanjaro epitomizes this, and to contemplate Kilimanjaro is also to contemplate the transience of human life. In a striking passage from *Green Hills of Africa*, Hemingway tells us – with a deliberately jarring mixture of mundane and lyrical metaphors – that 'the worn light bulbs of our discoveries and the empty condoms of our great loves float with no significance against one single, lasting thing – the stream.' According to him, art is the one human creation that has a chance of resisting the stream.

But enough of metaphor. East Africa, as Hemingway makes vivid in *Green Hills of Africa*, was a sensuously real land where he had the opportunity to live to the full, 'not just let my life pass'. Looking back on my journey in his footsteps, I now think I came closest to Hemingway in Africa neither while hunting leopards, nor in interviewing people who knew him, nor while driving through his green hills. I was actually closest to it when I seized the country with my own hands and lived it for myself.

Waking in the very early morning, waiting for coffee and for the day to begin, offers Africa at its most sublime. On one of the last mornings of my safari, by Lake Naivasha, I heard the morning chorus – the fish eagles crying to each other over the water, the cooing of the mourning doves, the hideous shriek of the hadada ibis and the melody of the African boubou. Long streaks of sunlight cast equally long shadows through the acacias onto the glistening grasses and dark papyrus by the water's edge. Above me, the sky was a hazy grey, waiting to turn blue... There are few places on earth so idyllic. Africa in the morning promises the world. It is a place and a time where the idea of becoming one's best self and achieving one's best work seems attainable.

BEWITCHED BY
THE SYRIAN DESERT

I shall return to the East, Inshallah! to end my
days there. Fortunately my husband has had the
same mind from his youth.

Isabel Burton,
The Inner Life of Syria, Palestine,
and the Holy Land, 1875

THE GREAT AND SCANDALOUS Sir Richard Burton – Victorian
explorer, anthropologist, Orientalist and translator of Arabian
erotica – is one of my driving influences. I have read everything he
wrote, except, of course, the papers notoriously incinerated by his
widow. I have tracked his footsteps half-way around the world. And
I have written two books about him. *Sindh Revisited* traces his early
wandering life in what is now Pakistan; *Journey to the Source of the*
Nile follows his ill-fated journey with John Hanning Speke to find
the headwaters of the world's longest river.

However, until 2009 I had never visited Syria, where Burton spent
two intense years as Her Majesty's consul from 1869 to 1871 with his
adoring wife Isabel. They were the turning point of his life.
Nicknamed the Emperor and Empress of Damascus, the Burtons
reached their zenith in Syria – before his cruelly abrupt recall by the
Foreign Office for upsetting one too many powerful local interests.

Unfortunately, the reader finds little of his Syrian romance in his
writings. But happily Isabel, in her private journal published as *The*
Inner Life of Syria, Palestine, and the Holy Land in 1875, gives us the

magic. After riding home into Damascus from the desert, she wrote: 'It was evening. First of all we saw a belt of something dark lining the horizon; then we entered by degrees under the trees, the orchards, and the gardens. We smelt the water from afar like a thirsty horse; we heard it gurgling long before we came to it; we scented and saw the limes, citrons and watermelons. We felt a mad desire to jump into the water, to eat our fill of fruit, to lie down and sleep under the delicious shade. At last we reached the door. The house seemed to me like a palace of comfort.'

The allure of Syria at last proved too much for me. But I did not want to go alone. Somehow, I convinced my wife Valda that together we should spend a little time experiencing something of what captivated Isabel Burton, along with other intrepid Englishwomen who lost their hearts to the Middle East, such as Lady Hester Stanhope (1776–1839), the first Western woman to visit the ruined oasis city of Palmyra, the much-married Lady Jane Digby El-Mezrab (1807–81), whose last husband was a Bedouin sheikh twenty years her junior, and Gertrude Bell (1868–1926), who worked with T. E. Lawrence in Aleppo and drew up the boundaries of the modern state of Iraq. My wife knew that we would have to stray a bit off the beaten track. 'Don't worry,' she said, adding Burton's often-quoted message to a stoic Isabel after he was sacked as consul: 'I will "pack and follow."'

Arriving in Damascus by air, we were collected by a driver who after tortuous circling dropped us near midnight in the Old Town. We walked a quarter of a mile along narrow cobbled streets to the ancient door of an exquisitely decorated courtyard – the entrance to the small Beit al-Mamlouka hotel. Though exhausted, we were already spellbound by the city, which is among the world's oldest continuously inhabited urban sites.

In the early morning, as on every morning we spent in Syria, we were woken by muezzins calling the faithful. I love the sound, just as Burton did; there was a mosque adjoining his house in Damascus.

Even if I did not get up, I would lie in bed listening, and think of all the things I could and should do. Early morning is when I get my best ideas.

There is a lot to see in Damascus, and we walked for miles and miles, constantly aware of past imperial influences: Amorite, Egyptian, Aramaean, Assyrian, Chaldean, Persian, Greek, Roman and Byzantine. The first Islamic caliphate, the Umayyad, made its capital here. The Umayyad Mosque, Damascus's most impressive building and Islam's holiest place after Mecca and Jerusalem's Dome of the Rock, was constructed by Caliph al-Walid in the early eighth century. When we visited – my wife clothed in a grey full-length robe and a headscarf, and our guide carrying my sandals so my hands were free for photography – we saw groups of religious scholars deep in debate, as well as pilgrims praying towards Mecca. But there were also families picnicking in the shade of the covered perimeter of the vast courtyard, happy to escape the clamour of the streets.

Disappointingly, no trace remains of the Burton house in the hill village of Salihiyya, now a suburb of Damascus, nor of the apricot orchards mentioned by Isabel. But in the Protestant cemetery near Bab al-Sharqi, we found the grave of the Burtons' intimate friend Jane Digby, a marble tomb with her name on the side. Three mysterious words, written by her Bedouin husband, are chiselled at the foot. They spell her title and name in Arabic. I recalled reading how in 1871, with tears in her eyes, Jane rode with a desolate Isabel to the gates of the city to bid her companion farewell.

We too were keen to escape into the desert, following the Burtons' 150-mile journey on horseback from Damascus to Palmyra, a 'splendid city of the dead rising out of, and half buried in, a sea of sand', wrote Isabel. Her husband's main reason for going there was 'his private wish to explore', but it was also his official duty to open up the country, 'now infested with hordes of wild Bedouin tribes, who attacked, robbed, and killed right and left'. We may have been travelling by jeep, not horses; but I was determined to meet some Bedouin nomads.

Before a brilliant desert sunset, after a day spent among Palmyra's spectacular Roman pillars and arches, I went with our guide to an isolated Bedouin camp a few miles away. We approached slowly and respectfully on foot. The first tent housed a sheep herder whose wife was milking their flock. After a friendly conversation, the herdsman allowed photography. His wife and two children stayed in the background. But at a second camp a younger woman talked enthusiastically and apparently humorously. Was I looking for a Bedouin wife? I said I was already married. She said that didn't matter, she could negotiate the purchase of a young bride. A figure of $200,000 was mentioned. 'Don't worry about the price', my guide explained. 'These things are always negotiable, if you are interested.' There was laughter all round. I got the feeling she was negotiating for herself. I knew that Jane Digby had spent some of her happiest times around Palmyra with her husband's tribe, the Mezrabis.

From Palmyra, we passed through empty desert, via Homs and Hama (ancient Epiphania), famous for its giant waterwheels still turned by the Orontes River, to Aleppo. As ancient as Damascus, Aleppo had become the third city of the Ottoman Empire after Istanbul and Cairo by the sixteenth century. Not until the opening of the Suez Canal in 1869, when Burton was consul, did Aleppo begin crumbling into a relic. Today, though, sensitive and imaginative architectural restoration with funds from the Syrian government and the Aga Khan Foundation has restored Aleppo's pride in its past. We stayed in a hotel converted from a lavish sixteenth-century palace.

The city's most famous sight is its souk, teeming with shoppers, travellers, donkeys and varied scents. It winds for an amazing ten miles, roofed with a stone vault with openings to admit light and air. We enjoyed at least three hours here buying *dishdashas* (long tunics), necklaces, old scarves and curios, including a stone falcon and an old

Syrian knife for my collection. I haggled over an intricately carved silver and lapis necklace for my wife until the store-owner, with resignation, asked me: 'Why are you arguing over a few Syrian pounds when your tall, slim, beautiful wife has an extraordinary South Sea pearl necklace around her neck?' I paid his price.

Despite Aleppo's excitements, we had to get back to Damascus where we had two appointments with the past before our final departure. We wanted to see Jane Digby's house; also, to talk our way into the old British Consulate where Burton held court for two years.

Her house, tucked away outside the Old City walls, was formerly surrounded by orchards and gardens. She designed, built and furnished it herself in classic Damascus style, with a high octagonal ceiling decorated with European wallpaper. The ceiling is there, though with hardly any wallpaper; and ornate wood cupboards are still set into the walls. The building is divided among thirty different families and in a terrible state. The current owners of the main part, who were extremely hospitable to us, keep a portrait of Lady Jane over their mantelpiece. At the old Consulate, by contrast, inside the Old City, there is no sign of Burton, yet the wonderful courtyard and magnificent gilt reception room where he must have received visitors are excellently preserved. The Aga Khan Foundation is considering turning the building into another small hotel.

Our days in Syria had been rushed but enthralling. As we packed with regret, I felt I could understand just a twinge of the Burtons' anguish when forced to leave Syria forever. It was a sad moment when I put my boots, still clouded with the dust of the desert, into my suitcase. My heart is still out there with the nomadic ghost of Richard Burton.

BLOOD LIBEL:
RICHARD BURTON AND
HUMAN SACRIFICE

*His dress and appearance were those suggesting
a released convict . . . a rusty black coat with a
crumpled black silk stock, his throat destitute of
collar, a costume which his muscular frame and
immense chest made singularly and incongruously
hideous, above it a countenance the most sinister
I have ever seen, dark, cruel, treacherous, with
eyes like a wild beast's. [Burton] reminded me of
a black leopard, caged, but unforgiving.*

Wilfrid Blunt,
*My Diaries: Being a Personal Narrative
of Events 1888–1914*, 1919

IN 2001, THE LONDON OFFICE of the auction house Christie's
telephoned me with the news that an explosive unpublished manuscript by Sir Richard Burton was to be sold in June that year.
Christie's added that the publishing rights might also be available.
This surprising information whetted my appetite, because almost all
of Burton's unpublished work was burnt by his widow, Isabel, after
his death in 1890.

The manuscript offered for sale by Christie's, 'Human Sacrifice
and the Sephardine or Eastern Jews', was well known to Burton

scholars. It had been owned by the Board of Deputies of British Jews since 1909. They had suppressed it, after an attempt at publication in about 1908, for fear that it might spark anti-Semitism as a result of Burton's claims about Jewish ritual murder. Having studied the manuscript myself, I agree that its anti-Semitism is beyond dispute, which it combines with passages of self-justification, some criticism of British statesmen (including Lord Palmerston), and the pursuit of anthropological and ethnographic facts. Nonetheless, it is an extraordinary work. I decided that I should try to buy it and publish it.

Christie's described the manuscript of over three hundred pages as follows:

> The unpublished chapters describe the events surrounding the disappearance of Padre Tomaso, a Capuchin friar, and his Syrian Christian servant, in Damascus in 1840, when thirteen members of the Jewish community were arrested and accused of having committed ritual murder. Some 'confessed' under torture, but all were eventually acquitted . . . Burton gives his views on the continuity of 'the tradition of human sacrifice', with an historical speech of accusations made in Syria, Lebanon and parts of Europe . . . The accusation of ritual murder made against the Jews was largely mentioned in Origen, and had parallels in charges made against various heretical Christian sects. The common form of it was the notion that at the Passover Christian blood was used in Jewish rites.

Burton, by relying on a dubious account of the trial of the thirteen Jews written by Achille Laurent, published in Paris in 1846, sought to reopen the accusation of ritual murder. His stance was obviously related to his bitterness at being dismissed from the post he loved as British consul in Damascus in 1871. His recall had been prompted by complaints from the Sublime Porte (the Ottoman court at

Constantinople) to the British ambassador in Constantinople about Burton's unauthorized wanderings and his denunciations of Muslim treatment of Christians. Burton, however, believed that his dismissal owed more to complaints by three Sephardic Jews that he 'had lost the composure befitting the Diplomatic Service'.

He completed writing the manuscript in Trieste in May 1872, and tried hard to get it published. But by 1877 he seems to have been dissuaded by friends, who feared the damage it might do to his reputation. There is little doubt that publication would have thrown a completely new and unflattering light on its author.

Isabel Burton left instructions for the manuscript to be burnt after her death in 1896. The story of its survival and subsequent fate are interesting and eventful, as described in detail by Priscilla Thomas, consultant on manuscripts at Christie's.

The trustees of Isabel's will included her nephew, Gerald Arthur Arundell (15th Baron Arundell of Wardour); her sister, Mrs Elizabeth Fitzgerald; and her secretary, Miss Plowman. According to Isabel's instructions, her and her husband's letters, journals and manuscripts were to be burnt by Miss Plowman. However, this destruction was postponed so that Isabel's editor, W. H. Wilkins, might use them to complete her autobiography (published posthumously).

Miss Plowman did not get Burton's manuscript back after lending it to Wilkins, and in 1901 she wrote that she could not recall whether it was included in the list of those to be burnt or not. 'If it was, it has already been consigned to the flames as I had the burning of the papers and carried out Lady Burton's instructions minutely.' A few years later, in 1908, she stated: 'I know that Lady Burton did not wish it to be published and certainly join with my co-trustees in strongly objecting to its publication.'

In fact, contrary to Miss Plowman's view, her co-executor Elizabeth Fitzgerald, Isabel's sister, was eager for publication of the manuscript. In the year after Isabel's death, 1897, the *Athenaeum* carried an advertisement for a forthcoming publication by Hutchinson and Co. of a work by Burton entitled *Human Sacrifice amongst the Eastern Jews: or the murder of Padre Tomaso*, edited by Wilkins. This caused great concern, especially at the Board of Deputies of British Jews, who opposed publication of a work that would 'revive a cruel and absurd medieval legend' and inflame racial hatred.

Threatened by a libel action, the publishers withdrew the book. Wilkins then deleted the more controversial chapters and published what remained as *The Jews, The Gypsy and El Islam* in 1898. Then, in the words of Priscilla Thomas herself,

> In 1904 Wilkins, whose ownership of the manuscript was doubtful, gave it to the antiquarian bookseller Sotherans. They sold it to Henry Manners-Sutton, who in 1908 approached Gerald Arundell [Isabel Burton's nephew] for permission to reprint certain passages. But Arundell and his co-executors objected strongly and in 1909 the ownership of the manuscript and of all the rights in it were transferred by deed of assignment to David Lido Alexander KC, who was President of the Board of Deputies. Mr Manners-Sutton gave up the manuscript only after a ruling in the High Court, on 27 March 1911, which ordered him to surrender it.

Note that the assignment in 1909 to David Alexander, who was then chairman of the trustees of the Board of Deputies as well as its president, included 'all the rights' in the manuscript. This is why, in June 2001, the trustees of the Board of Deputies believed that they were selling not only the manuscript but also the right to publish the manuscript, including the copyright.

When the bidding at Christie's started at £90,000, I topped the bid at £100,000. Then I bid £120,000, and went on to £130,000. And then suddenly, standing in the auction room, I began to have second thoughts. Burton himself had been dissuaded from allowing the controversial manuscript to be published in 1877. Isabel had been determined in her will that the work should be burnt after her death in 1896. A second attempt by Wilkins had been thwarted by Isabel Burton's executors in 1897 and again in 1908. Why should the book be given worldwide readership now? Perhaps it would be better for it to be acquired by a responsible institution like the Huntington Library in California. Or indeed to remain with the Board of Deputies of British Jews.

The bidding stood at £140,000. The estimated reserve price was £150,000. One more bid from me – and the manuscript would have been mine to publish as I saw fit. But I stopped. The manuscript was not sold. It remained the property of the Board of Deputies. For the time being, at least, Burton's reputation would remain free of the charge of virulent anti-Semitism.

However, the story of the manuscript did not stop there. It has a significant further chapter. In 2006, I was urged by Sir Sigmund Sternberg, chairman of the Sternberg Foundation, to approach the Board of Deputies once more. He was sympathetic to my argument that Burton's perplexing work should be published – alongside explicit counter-arguments by scholars showing that Burton was obsessed with black sexuality, believed in Jewish ritual murder and was indeed a 'scurrilous racist' – a view shared by Tony Kushner, the Marcus Sieff Professor of Jewish and Non-Jewish Relations at Southampton University.

On the other hand, another prominent British Jew, a former president of the Board of Deputies in the 1980s, Greville Janner, now Lord Janner of Braunstone, was consistently unsympathetic to publication of the Burton manuscript. In a memoir he published in 2008 he wrote: 'Sir Richard Burton was a famous nineteenth-century explorer . . . He was also a raging anti-Semite who . . . penned an attempted justification of the blood libel accusations against the

Jews.' The desire of the Board of Deputies to sell the manuscript in 2001, in order to raise money to buy new premises, 'outraged' its former president. In an interview with BBC Television's *Newsnight* programme at the time of the auction, Lord Janner expressed the view that 'for the Board to put this anti-Semitic document on sale was a grotesque error'.

So it was with some trepidation that I subsequently telephoned Henry Grunwald QC, the current president of the Board of Deputies of British Jews, to plead for my strongly held belief that the Burton manuscript should be published, under the supervision of the Board, with an introduction, a historical account of its writing and reception, and a scholarly commentary on its contents. Although he listened politely, Grunwald was quite firm that neither the release of the manuscript for public scrutiny nor its publication would be possible, because someone had recently made a considerable donation to a separate trust administered by the Board of Deputies of British Jews to ensure that Burton's manuscript would never again be considered for sale. In the words of a follow-up statement from the Board of Deputies,

> The manuscript is now owned by a private trust, although it is possible for genuine scholars to have access to it for legitimate research purposes. The common view is that it contains irredeemably outmoded and racist views, which the current owners see no reason to publicise. This was indeed the position adopted by the Executors of Lady Burton's Estate, although no doubt one of their concerns was to protect the author's reputation.

The Burton manuscript will not be destroyed. It will remain intact, under lock and key in the safe of the Board of Deputies of British Jews in London. But, almost as certainly, it will never now be published. Burton's legacy has been protected, as his wife indubitably wanted. Which outcome – suppression or publication of the manu-script – would have satisfied the controversial and enigmatic author himself, is impossible to determine.

THE RISE AND FALL
OF NATHANIEL NAISMITH

*Money ... has often been a cause of the delusion
of multitudes ... Men, it has been well said, think
in herds; it will be seen that they go mad in herds,
while they only recover their senses slowly, and
one by one.*

> Charles Mackay,
> *Extraordinary Popular Delusions and
> the Madness of Crowds*, 1852

WHEN I DECIDED to uncover the secrets of the seven years
(1842–49) that Richard Burton spent in India, in 1993, I knew my
work was cut out for me. I would follow in Burton's footsteps over
thousands of miles, trekking across deserts where ancient tribes meet
modern civilization in the valley of the mighty Indus River. There
were numerous individuals I wanted to meet in Pakistan, and I had
hopes that they would lead to many other unscheduled encounters.
But I certainly never expected, on the morning of my very first day,
to bump into an old business acquaintance from Canada now living
in Pakistan. Not only that, he turned out to have a penchant for
Burton, too.

It happened at the Sind Club in Karachi, the capital of the province
of what is now spelt Sindh. The Sind Club was founded in 1871 with
seventy-six inaugural members, all British civil servants. Pakistani
and Indian members were accepted only in the early 1950s. Today

there are nearly two thousand members, some of them residents of the club. The clubhouse, completed in 1883, is a grand building. Long, low porches stretch away on either side of a main entrance portico, and a balconied second storey runs the entire width of the building. In the grounds there are elegant gardens, tennis and squash courts, and attentive servants. Everything is protected from the turmoil of Karachi behind high walls and a large black wrought-iron gate. The club quickly proved to be a haven for my turbulent research on Burton.

I had arrived from London in the small hours, around 1.30 a.m. There had been little chance for sleep. At dawn, the muezzin had called the faithful to prayer in the city. A multitude of crows, kites and even a few falcons were soaring overhead and making a commotion outside my window. Then, at 6.15 a.m., a tall, elderly club bearer had appeared, dressed totally in white in long pajamas with a fez-like hat embroidered in red with the motto 'Sind Club'. Mohammed Younus was very apologetic at the earliness of the hour, but he had a message for me. After I had asked him for some strong coffee, he produced a card with the words 'Nathaniel Naismith, Assistant Manager, Sind Club' printed on it. The name seemed to ring a bell somewhere in my mind, but I thought this was probably just a formal introduction or welcome from the club.

'Mr Manager wants to see you, Sir. After breakfast.' Younus tried to explain further in English, then gave up the struggle. So I said 'Fine. OK. Eleven o'clock.' '*Achcha*', he replied.

I spent the first part of the first morning on my research notes, then sauntered around the clubhouse. The furnishings were in the colonial style, with the silver cups and trophies typical of colonial clubs in my childhood in Ceylon. There was a verandah attached to the dining room, overlooking the garden, and a drawing room, bridge room, reading room and cocktail bar. However, no liquor was served anywhere in the club, as Karachi was officially dry. Nor was

I allowed to take photographs. It seemed like a world within a world – unrelated to the modern city.

At 11 a.m. I made my way to the club offices. The moment I stepped in, I recognized him, and was transported back a quarter of a century. To Toronto, 1969, to be precise. Nathaniel Naismith – of course. It all came flooding back, even some of the financial details.

He and I were in the same stockbroking firm, Pitfield Mackay Ross and Company. I was then in my mid-thirties and worked in the newly formed institutional broking division. Naismith was at least ten years older and head of the stock-trading desk. Although he was English and schooled at Winchester, he had been to McGill University in Montreal before joining Pitfield. We overlapped for a few years in the 1960s. Although we were never friends, from time to time we used to talk.

The trading desk and floor were rough places in those days. Millions of dollars swapped hands throughout the day and every-thing was done by word of mouth through a multitude of telephone lines. The system worked, and it worked efficiently. I remembered Naismith as being quite powerful in the firm. He controlled the trading desk with a rod of steel. He alone made the decisions, with the complete confidence of the senior directors. He drank with the traders after work and no doubt settled some nasty situations in the Nag's Head, or the Oak Room, or Winston's, or any of the local watering holes on Bay or King Street. He was well paid, married, and rumoured to be keeping a part-Chinese mistress somewhere east of the King Edward Hotel.

Then he got a big break. Pitfield Mackay Ross underwrote a new Canadian company, Velok Ltd., which in 1957 had entered into a licensing agreement with a Swiss company, Velcro S.A., to produce and distribute Velcro tape in the western hemisphere as well as Asia and the Pacific. Velcro fasteners are now famous, but few people know that Velcro was the invention of George de Mestral. In 1941, while walking his dog in some Alpine countryside, he noticed that cockleburs continually fastened themselves to his trousers. Examining them under a microscope, he found multiple tiny hooks on the surface of each bur and loops of fabric on his trousers. He appreciated the application of the discovery right away, but it took him eight years of tinkering to perfect a manufacturing process.

Some smart investors bought the stock soon after Velok went public in 1959. By the mid-1960s, when Velok changed its name to Velcro, sales were approaching $10 million a year, with the shares trading at between $31 and $32. I remembered buying some shares in 1965 with whatever meagre funds I had available. I would certainly have bought more if I had had more cash. Many of the directors of Pitfield, and its traders, had already taken hefty positions in the company. The stock continued to climb, when Velcro was used in the Apollo moonflight programme and airlines began using the Velcro fastener to keep seat pads in place. By late 1966, I recalled that Velcro stock was trading at an amazing $280, undaunted by a bear market. Many bold investors, including Naismith, borrowed against their increased portfolio value and bought yet more stock.

But, as always, if something seems too good to be true, it usually is. The market broke, like a taut wire snapping under too much strain. It happened in early June of 1969. All across Bay Street there were horrendous stories of personal bankruptcies. Naismith was one of the casualties.

And now here he was standing in front of me, offering his hand. Still short and quite stocky, but dressed in a safari suit, brown shoes and a club tie. 'Hello, Christopher. I saw your name on the member-guest list and I knew there couldn't be too many Ondaatjes around. I've been looking forward to seeing you. But do you remember me? A lot of water has passed under the bridge since those heady Bay Street days.'

'Of course I remember you. Who wouldn't? But then you disappeared. No one had any idea what had happened to you. Not even the directors. I guess you know that some of us left Pitfield Mackay Ross and started our own firm?'

'Oh yes. I've tried to keep in touch. But it's hard to get real news once you get off the train. Anyway, let's sit down. There's nothing to drink here, as you know. Not even a beer. So let's have a lime and soda. It's thirst-quenching and doesn't get you into trouble. Sometimes someone brings in a bottle of Black Label from abroad and we have a few snorts, but strictly in private. I hear you are right out of the financial world now, like me. I suppose I'm really a colonial, too. All that mumbo-jumbo stock-market stuff seems unreal now. It's a game that works only when everyone plays along. And when the music stops, some people get left without a chair to sit on. But I suppose I'm talking too much. What are you doing here?'

I told Naismith about my research on Burton in India. However, to be truthful, what I really wanted to hear about was what he was doing in Karachi.

'You know Burton was here in the 1840s when the original club was just a shack in the servants' quarters. When a competition was held to select the best design for the club, he warned against the use of Gothic architecture. He said that "the Veneto-Gothic, so fit for Venice, is so unfit for Karachi," or something like that. So when Le Mesurier was chosen to design the Club he must have taken Burton's advice. The first Sind Club building, which now houses the ladies' bar and dining room, was designed as you see in a southern Italianate style. The other blocks, which were constructed later, continued to follow an Indo-Italianate style. Thank God everything was set back from the road. One feels safe here. You know, for a long time, there used to be a large sign in front of the Club saying "Natives and dogs not allowed." It was removed only the day after Jinnah took his oath as governor-general of Pakistan in '47. How things have changed! But I think for the better.'

'When did you come here?' I interjected.

'Ah, that's a long story and I'm not sure you want to hear all of it.' He paused, then went on. 'You remember when Velcro collapsed. The banks, particularly the Royal Bank of Canada, called in my loans. I had to sell my stock. It didn't cover half of what I had borrowed, so I realized I was virtually bankrupt. Of course Pitfield and the board weren't particularly sympathetic, and I suppose the Royal Bank, as Pitfield's bankers, must have put pressure on the board to try to get some of their money back. I pleaded with the directors but they said I would have to sell whatever assets I had. That meant my house, car, everything. My wife left and went back to her parents in England, temporarily I thought, while I tried to sort things out. But it was impossible. Eventually I lost my job and even though they gave me a decent severance settlement, most of it went to the Royal Bank. Then I moved into a two-room apartment near King and Yonge Street with this girlfriend of mine. But that didn't last long. Frankly I was at my wits' end. No job, no money, nowhere to stay, and I still owed a hell of a lot of money. I tried to get another job but, if you remember the early 1970s in Canada, you know there was nothing going. Brokerage firms were laying off people left, right and centre.

'Finally, I went back to England and lived with my parents for a bit. My marriage at last broke up. I tried to get some kind of job in the City – no luck. God! It was a terrible time for me.

'And then, my father had an English friend of his from Citibank in Karachi for dinner and he said he could fix me up on the currency trading desk if I was prepared to go to Pakistan. Actually the Citibank job worked out quite well for a while, but trading currency isn't the same as being in charge of a large stock-trading operation. It's actually a completely different business. Everything is measured against the U.S. dollar or sterling and it was hard to keep up with the collapsing Eastern currencies – particularly the rupee. I just didn't understand the market.'

'So how did the club job come about?' I asked.

'I was a member anyway, which made things a bit easier. Everyone knew me. So in 1983, nearing retirement, I was offered this job at the club and I took it. It's a perfect job for me. I miss England sometimes, the Worcester Cricket Ground with the cathedral, Old Bosham and the sailing, the London theatre. But I don't miss Canada or Bay Street at all. My real mistake was believing too much in the system and the pieces of paper. I know it was wonderful while it lasted, but now it seems more like a nightmare. I've come to realize that nothing lasts forever, and I'm much more philosophical about success and failure. I guess you may have some idea what I am talking about, since you've chucked the Canadian financial scene too, to do something different. Burton has always been one of my heroes. I think you'll find much more here than you bargained for. Sindh shaped every aspect of Burton's life. It has changed me. My bet is that it'll change you too... But now I must get back to work. Members will be coming in for lunch soon. Look after yourself. Sindh can be an unruly place outside these club walls. Good luck, and let me know if there is anything I can do for you.'

I left him to his job, went off to the verandah of the club, and looked out at the immaculate gardens. A few members had already arrived for what looked like a business lunch. Naismith's rise and fall had disturbed me more than I cared to admit. With a different roll of the dice, I knew that something like this could easily have happened to me.

THE KILLING OF
SIR HARRY OAKES

I wanted the gold, and I sought it,
I scrabbled and mucked like a slave.
Was it famine or scurvy – I fought it;
I hurled my youth into a grave.
I wanted the gold, and I got it –
Came out with a fortune last fall, –
Yet somehow life's not what I thought it;
And somehow the gold isn't all.

Robert W. Service,
The Spell of the Yukon, 1907

THE DISCOVERY OF GOLD by Harry Oakes is one of the most incredible success stories in Canadian history. Although born in Maine in the United States and trained as a doctor, Oakes threw up everything to prospect for gold during the Klondike Gold Rush of 1897–98. For over ten years he toiled in paralysingly cold and blisteringly hot climates in Canada, Alaska, California and Australia before staking the richest half mile of gold in the world at Kirkland Lake in Northern Ontario in 1912. Eventually his Lakeshore Mines became the most productive mining company in the western hemisphere. By 1920, Oakes was one of the richest private citizens of Canada. But years of adversity had produced an abrasiveness in him that people found impossible to handle. In 1935, refusing to pay the exorbitant taxes levied on him by the Canadian government, he left the country and became a resident of the tax-free Bahamas. He also became a British subject, and was created a baronet in 1939 for his philanthropic deeds. It is estimated that Oakes took more than $300 million out of Canada when he left the country.

On 8 July 1943, Oakes was brutally murdered in his Bahamian mansion. In what looked like a ritual killing, he had been bludgeoned to death with an instrument that could have been an ice pick, and his body partially burned and strewn with feathers. A sensational trial took place, but no one was found guilty of the murder. The true killer or killers of Sir Harry Oakes have never been conclusively identified to this day. The Oakes murder is widely regarded as the greatest unsolved celebrity murder of all time.

In 2010, I had dinner at Mrs Sibilla Clark's villa Parco Flora in the Lyford Cay Club in the Bahamas. There were ten people at the table, including Lewis Lapham, the former editor of *Harper's Magazine*, Princess Michael of Kent, Colin Callender, a resident Bahamian, and Baron Alexander von Hoyningen-Huene. Colin Callender is the son of the lawyer Ernest Callender who defended Count Alfred de Marigny, the man charged with killing Oakes in 1943, while Baron 'Sasha' von Hoyningen-Huene is the son of Oakes's daughter Nancy by her second husband. Her first husband was Count de Marigny. Thus, it was inevitable that at some point during the evening the conversation would get around to the murder.

The responsibility for investigating the crime fell on the governor of the Bahamas. In 1943 he was the Duke of Windsor, the recently abdicated King Edward VIII. Refusing to use Scotland Yard detectives from England, which would have been the sensible decision, the duke instead hired two Americans from the Miami Police Force. Almost immediately the two detectives arrested Oakes's son-in-law, Count Alfred de Marigny, a twice-married playboy opportunist who had eloped with Oakes's eighteen-year-old daughter Nancy, creating a serious rift between the newly married couple and Sir Harry and

Lady Oakes. The young Nancy de Marigny stood by her husband during the sensational trial despite a general consensus that the count was guilty. Her evidence and dramatic courtroom appearance played a great part in her husband's acquittal, particularly as the incompetent American investigators, Captains Melcher and Barker, were exposed as having fabricated evidence against Marigny. Nevertheless, Marigny was deported from the Bahamas. He left New Providence Island for Cuba with his young wife to stay with his friend Ernest Hemingway. Three years later, Nancy left Marigny and they were divorced in 1949. She married Baron Hoyningen-Huene in 1952 and had a son, Alexander, who was my fellow guest at Sibilla Clark's dinner.

There have been numerous articles on the Oakes murder, and a number of books speculating on a solution to the unsolved crime. Geoffrey Bocca's *The Life and Death of Sir Harry Oakes* and John Marquis's *Blood and Fire* are inconclusive, but point to the possibility that the Miami mafia, ruled by Meyer Lansky, might have been hired by the would-be assassin or assassins to kill Oakes. *King of Fools* by John Parker theorizes that associates of Lansky murdered Oakes because he had blocked plans to introduce casino gambling in the Bahamas. Charles Higham, in *The Duchess of Windsor: The Secret Life*, is convinced that African ritual specialists were sent to Nassau by Oakes's real-estate partner Harold Christie to kill him. There is no doubt that Oakes and Christie had fallen out over a land deal for a new Royal Air Force base in the Bahamas.

There are other theories, too. Sir Hiram Maxim in *The Tale of Two Knights* recalls that Marigny, many years after his acquittal, claimed he had found one of the missing watchmen who were at the Oakes mansion on the night of the murder. The man had heard three or four gunshots and minutes later had seen flames coming from Sir Harry's bedroom. Two men then left the house in a sedan car. The watchman fled in terror – but not before he had identified a third man in the vehicle as Christie. As Marigny explained, Christie paid the watchmen £100 each to leave Nassau and never return. A local harbour master who had witnessed the arrival of a mysterious boat at about midnight on the night of the murder was reported drowned in the harbour. If Marigny's story that Oakes was shot, rather than bludgeoned to death, is true, then there should still be small-calibre bullets in the skull of Oakes, which lies in a crypt of the East Dover Cemetery in Dover-Foxcroft, Maine.

Marigny also exposed the fact that Christie had avoided the investigation because any competent inquiry would have revealed that he, along with Oakes and the Duke of Windsor, had conspired to smuggle millions of dollars out of the Bahamas in violation of currency regulations. As Maxim recounts, Oakes left a personal fortune valued at only $12 million, not including his real-estate assets. No satisfactory explanation has ever been given of what happened to the rest of his fortune, estimated to be something short of $300 million. Certainly the duke, as governor of the Bahamas, had the power to reopen the investigation, but he never used it.

Kirk Wilson's book, *Unsolved Crimes*, develops the mafia theory. Wilson theorizes that Charles 'Lucky' Luciano and his associate Lansky masterminded the idea of developing casinos in the Bahamas. The islands' three most prominent citizens – the Duke of Windsor, Sir Harry Oakes and Harold Christie – had the capacity to make or break the deal. When Oakes refused to take part in the enormous money-making scheme, Luciano and Lansky ordered his murder. Wilson even speculates that the Swedish industrial tycoon Axel Wenner-Gren and the Duke of Windsor became suspects in the Oakes murder after Marigny was acquitted. Both Wenner-Gren and the duke were suspected Nazi sympathizers. According to Wilson, Wenner-Gren may have had Oakes murdered because he knew too much about a secret Bahamas-based spy operation on behalf of Nazi Germany.

Most recently Jason Bennett, a reporter for the *Independent* news-paper in England, revealed in 2006 that secret files kept by Scotland Yard released to the *Independent* show that a certain Walter Foskett was the man responsible for the Oakes killing. An explosively important document sent to Scotland Yard by Charles Bates, the legal attaché at the American Embassy in London, on 10 June 1959 con-tained an FBI report of an interview with Fred Maloof, an art dealer from Maryland, who named Foskett as the man who arranged the murder. Foskett, a Miami lawyer, had been hired by Oakes to keep his fortune out of the clutches of the taxman. The FBI report con-tends that the unscrupulous Foskett was almost certainly swindling Oakes and that Sir Harry was murdered in the wake of a stormy meeting in Miami when Oakes confronted Foskett. Furthermore, the files show that Nancy Oakes, now remarried with the title of Baroness von Hoyningen-Huene, tried and failed to get the case reopened. On 25 May 1959, in a letter to the attorney general of the Bahamas, she stated: 'At the time of my father's death, it would appear that no investigation was in fact made, except around the personality of Alfred de Marigny.'

On the morning after Sibilla Clark's dinner I had a meeting in Old Fort with Orjan Lindroth, the son of Arne Lindroth, who was Wenner-Gren's manager in the Bahamas.

'Impossible!' he said. 'There has never been a shred of evidence that Wenner-Gren was a Nazi sympathizer. *Call to Reason*, a book written by Wenner-Gren and published in Europe before the Oakes murder, was extremely critical of the events in Europe and the Nazi party. And there is no way he could have killed Oakes because he was in Mexico at the time of the murder.' As Lindroth explained, 'Wenner-Gren was first and foremost a capitalist. He had millions tied up in business in Europe. As you know, he was the founder of the Electrolux vacuum cleaner and refrigerator company. Europe in the early 1940s was in a mess and Wenner-Gren realized that the only haven for a capitalist like him was America. He was a major shareholder of the Bank of the Bahamas, which at that time was an off-shore holding company and not an operating bank. Later, when he was blacklisted and all his assets in the Bahamas were frozen, he moved to Mexico and acquired a bank. The blacklisting eroded his personal fortune and shortly after his death in 1960 from cancer his estate became insolvent. In the aftermath, the Swedish government conducted a forensic audit of his affairs to try to understand where his money went. They found no evidence of any illegal money transfers. On the contrary, he was in debt to Swedish banks and had borrowed heavily to support his personal expenditure.'

In Lindroth's view, all of the books on the Oakes murder amount to nothing more than hearsay and speculation. 'I don't think any author did any kind of detailed research on the island. Perhaps Marigny, or others, killed Oakes. Or perhaps the mob in Miami. But not Wenner-Gren. There was no motive for him.'

Two days after our dinner, I cornered Sasha von Hoyningen-Huene and asked him whether he could shed even a ray of new light on the murder. 'Listen, Christopher', he finally said to me awkwardly. 'The truth is that no one knows and no one will ever know the whole truth. But there are a few things that are seldom talked about. The first is that my grandfather was an important senior figure in MI6 during the war, working for the British cause. He was a real patriot. I was told this by Wing Commander Robert Carr. It is conceivable that my grandfather was killed because he knew something that would have exposed Nazi activity in the Bahamas and possibly North America. The Duke of Windsor is known to have had Nazi sympathies, as did his wife, the former Mrs Wallis Simpson.

'Secondly, my mother tried very hard to get the case reopened in 1959. She was absolutely convinced that her former husband, Count Alfred de Marigny, was not her father's murderer. However, what not many people know is that my grandfather had an elder sister,

Gertrude, who had great faith in the young Oakes when he was prospecting for gold and who sent him a little bit of money from time to time whenever she could while she was in Washington working as a clerk in some government department. After Oakes struck it rich at Kirkland Lake in 1912, it was Gertrude who looked after the administrative side of the mining operation. My grandfather totally trusted his sister. After all, it was a family business. It was only when she died tragically in an ocean liner collision off New York that the administrative nightmare of the Oakes empire really began. Somehow my mother, by then married to my father, learned about the dealings between her father and Walter Foskett, who was a really unsavoury character. She herself told me that she thought Foskett had been involved in the murder. It is known that my grandfather changed his will shortly before he died and my understanding is that he made Walter Foskett a trustee of his will. Everybody suspected Foskett of cheating my grandfather and it is known that he questioned Foskett about his shady dealings only a few days before he was killed.

'One last piece of advice. This is not 1943, nor even the 1950s. But as you know, many people who have tried to dig up the truth about the Harry Oakes murder have come to a sticky end. In the sixteen years following the Oakes murder, no fewer than sixteen people were killed who were either directly or indirectly involved in the crime. One female reporter who came close to the truth and boasted about it refused to heed warnings and her body was found upside down in a banana hole. Other witnesses were threatened off the island. The senior head of police in the Bahamas found out a little too much and was immediately transferred to Trinidad. He died years later, still refusing to say anything about what he had discovered. Books have been written as well as articles, but there is always the danger that some clever writer could put himself or herself in a position of knowing too much. Be careful what you say, and what you write.'

As a long-time visitor to the Bahamas, I know that the killing of Oakes on that stormy night of 1943 casts a dark shadow over these islands. Even as I try to piece together the extraordinary story, I cannot avoid a frisson of fear. Because of this brutal and bizarre unsolved murder, the idyllic atmosphere of the Bahamas continues to have a dark undercurrent of violence and mystery.

SARGENT'S ASHES

The Knight's bones are dust,
And his good sword rust; –
His soul is with the saints, I trust.

Samuel Taylor Coleridge,
'The Knight's Tomb', *c.* 1817

TOBY CLIFFORD is a great friend of mine. He lives practically next door to Devon, in Somerset, only sixteen miles away from me in an old Victorian rectory on the Barle River near Dulverton. We've got used to travelling down to the West Country together from London, taking the 9.06 a.m. train from Paddington that arrives in Taunton at 11.47 a.m., give or take a few minutes, depending on whether there are 'leaves on the line', 'signal repairs' or some other excuse. Generally speaking, the journey takes a little less than two hours, and we get home in time for lunch, after going our separate ways at Taunton.

I remember one of these journeys particularly well. It was in July, and I had just finished writing the last of the short stories in this book and was feeling quite pleased with myself. In fact, I could hardly contain my enthusiasm as I began telling my travelling companion about the collection. I knew that Toby had already read a few of the pieces that had been published in magazines such as the *Spectator*, *Country Life* and the *Traveller*. So he knew roughly what I was up to.

Besides being a good listener, he is also a very entertaining travel-ling companion. My wife and I had taken him, with his wife, to the

West Indian island of Barbuda in 2003, where we had a marvellous time. We had been there many times before, so I showed Toby and his wife everything I could about the island, which was leased from the British Crown from 1685 to 1870 by the Codrington family as a slave 'nursery' and is still owned by the neighbouring island of Antigua. After their emancipation in 1834, Barbuda's former slaves became tenants of the Crown and fiercely protected their right to the land: only Barbudans can own land in Barbuda, which is given to them free of charge. Together we visited the mighty palmetto-forested Darby's Cave; the Indian cave on the windswept north-east with its petroglyphs; the ruins of the old Codrington mansion on the highest hill of the island; and the coral reefs at Spanish Point, in the south-east corner of Barbuda. And I kept the best until last: the frigate bird nesting colony at the north end of an enormous lagoon surrounded by mangroves – the largest frigate bird gathering in the world, with over 2,500 birds, many of them males blowing up their scarlet throats to attract female mates. An amazing sight. We stayed at Coco Point Lodge, a secluded paradise on its own 164-acre peninsula bordered by miles of pink and white sand. It is one of the least discovered hideaways in the Caribbean. We did nothing but read, eat well, drink good wines, swim, laze in the sun and explore when we felt like it.

Sadly, the trip wrecked my friend's marriage. Sarah Clifford literally fell in love with the West Indies and out of love with her husband. We didn't know about it then, and neither did he. 'You know,' he said, 'it was the strangest thing. I didn't know what was happening to us. We got back to England and she started selling all her things. Everything that belonged to her. The silver, the paintings off the wall, the first-edition books, her grandfather's watercolours. Even some of her jewelry, although that she kept till the very end. She didn't talk much about what she was doing. She was very silent and our relationship was very different from what it had been before.

Our son Peter, who was just getting ready to go to Cambridge, wondered what on earth was going on. It was a very difficult time, and things were never the same again.

'And then Hurricane Ivan hit the southern coastline of Jamaica, quite near where you had taken us on Barbuda. It was only a category four hurricane but it ravaged villages and caused considerable injury to communities. Many, many people were displaced or homeless. Jamaica needed aid and the University Hospital of the West Indies advertised for help. Sarah jumped into action immediately. She took money, clothes, whatever she could, and got on one of the earliest aid transports to Kingston. It's almost as if she was waiting for the disaster to happen. And you know the rest. She stayed in Jamaica. She's been back and forth a few times but lives there now. Just chucked all her responsibilities here, our marriage, the house, Peter and his university – skipped the Western world and disappeared into the Caribbean. I've hardly seen her. It was a tough thing sorting out the divorce, the property, and coming to terms with the life I'm leading now. It's been lonely. I've virtually had to start all over again, and that's not really something I've wanted to do. It still isn't, and I'm living in a completely different world where I don't have anyone to share things with. It isn't me.'

Toby paused for a moment. 'Well, that's enough of that. Why I'm telling you this is that your literary project and your hardly contained enthusiasm compel me to tell you a rather strange story arising from my break-up.

'Sarah took everything of hers she cared about, except the ashes of her American father, Sargent Whitney. These she left in their original casket, with specific instructions that the ashes be distributed in France. That's all. But I didn't do anything about it until April of last year. God knows why she'd given me this particular final task. It preyed on my mind, particularly when I was clearing out the house to sell up. Perhaps she thought it would bring me closer to my son.

In London, the wretched box haunted my mantelpiece for months. But then a plan began to hatch in my mind. I decided that if I was going to distribute my father-in-law's ashes in France, I was damn well going to do the job properly.

'You see, I knew Sargent Whitney in person only a little, but I knew masses about his life from Sarah. He was certainly a character. Born in France, distinguished during the Second World War, multilingual, a professional diplomat who lived much of his life with an extremely wealthy, rather spoilt American princess officially married to a husband who was, to put it mildly, not heterosexual. She eventually left him for Sargent, bought a French château for them both to live in, and never went back to the United States. Well, in honour of Sargent's adventures, I decided to take our son Peter with me to France, visit Sargent's old haunts, and distribute a portion of his ashes in every one of his favourite places. This proved to be quite challenging, as I'll explain, but I liked the idea. Not only would I fulfil my responsibility, it would also give me a chance to show Peter something of the unusual life his grandfather had enjoyed.'

I was now listening to Toby intently. Here is the 'rather strange' story he told me, entirely in his own words. I was so intrigued by it that I stole it for my just-completed book.

'I realized that we couldn't go throwing mortal remains indiscriminately in places like the Bar Vendôme in the Ritz in Paris, or Maxim's restaurant, or the courtyard of the Talleyrand buildings on Rue St-Florentin that housed the American Embassy Consular Services, or indeed the Gothic loftiness of Notre-Dame Cathedral where Napoleon crowned himself emperor. We had to be discreet, even a bit furtive.

'We took the train from London to avoid any problems with airport security. The casket and its contents looked a bit too much like badly cut drugs or even cocaine, we thought. In Paris we stayed in a small hotel in the Latin Quarter on the Left Bank – a place where Sargent would definitely *not* have stayed. He was much more of a Right Bank man. We arrived at midday, had lunch, and watched some football on television while we decanted Sargent's remains into half a dozen small cloth bags, which fitted into our blazer and trouser pockets. The casket was too noticeable to carry around.

'Around dusk on that first evening we set out, looking quite well dressed. In fact, I can't remember when I last saw Peter wearing a tie. Our first stop was the Hôtel Lotti near the Louvre, between the Place Vendôme and the Tuileries Gardens. This is where Sargent would usually stay on his frequent trips to Paris from the château in the Loire where he lived with his mistress. Heading for the luxurious bar, we sat on the tall bar stools and ordered ourselves two large dry Martinis – that was Sargent's drink – and as we sat there toasting him, we dribbled ashes onto the richly patterned carpet. This took the best part of half an hour.

'Then, emboldened by our first act, and by the gin, we moved around the Place Vendôme to the bar of the Ritz where we ordered even drier Martinis. As we drank, I told Peter some of the stories about Sargent I had heard from Peter's mother and her friends. He was said to have been served the very last lunch at the Ritz before the arrival of the German army in 1940. He was dining with a French friend, an art critic. There were only two people in the restaurant, and when Sargent asked for the bill, the *maître d'hotel* said they would settle it after the war. So we sprinkled some ashes in what is now the Hemingway Bar and then, fortified, went into the gloriously floodlit courtyard and put more ashes into the baroque fountains. We sprinkled some, too, on the glass tops of the corridor cabinets bursting with opulent trinkets. Then, a bit guiltily, we ran down the corridors and left the hotel.

'The Bristol Hotel received some more of Sargent's remains, but this time we dropped them in the enormous vases at the foot of the foyer steps and at the foot of the topiary by the hotel entrance with its white façade on the Rué du Faubourg St-Honoré. However the white Carrara marble floors, the Baccarat crystal chandeliers, and the Savonnerie rugs in muted green and royal blue made us feel nervous, so we retreated to a late dinner in Montmartre. As we climbed into a taxi, Peter whispered: "I have some left, Dad." I said: "Keep it. We have a big day tomorrow."

'Getting up very early on the second day we made our way to the Gare d'Austerlitz and caught the fast train to Tours in the Loire. From there we headed to the Château de La Bourdaisière in Montlouis-sur-Loire, which had been owned by Christina, Sargent's mistress. Though built in the fifteenth century, it has a sixteenth-century Renaissance façade, extensively altered at the end of the nineteenth century, with a huge conical water tower erected in 1907. Around the three-storey building there are rose-clad stables and two *pigeonniers*, not to mention a pair of symmetrically designed lakes. A lovely setting, but here our mission faced a problem: the château was closed. The caretakers, along with the rest of the village, had gone to the local *fête*. We had to come back again the next day, or scale an eight-foot perimeter wall at the rear of the grounds. We could hear the guard dogs barking, but that didn't stop us.

'Inside the grounds there was a young beech tree in a glade. Here we made our first deposit of the day – a generous one, directly from Sargent's casket. Nearby were the remnants of his private maze I had also heard about, a symbol of a bygone era of wealth and excess. Throwing caution to the winds, we stepped into the open, approached the château, and stopped at a gnarled oak through which grew a rambling rose planted by Sargent when he had first moved to the château. We made another liberal deposit at the base of its trunk. Moving still closer, and ignoring my son's over-enthusiastic plea to swim in the swimming pool, we came to the edge of one of the lakes. Peter scattered a cloud of his grandfather's ashes on the still surface of the water. Immediately, two large carp swirled up and fought over the remains. We felt it was time to go, before the guard dogs came for us in earnest. It began to rain as we climbed into the safety of our tiny rented Peugeot.

'That night we stayed in a small, quiet *auberge* on the banks of the Loire. We felt happy with what we were doing for Sargent. We thought he would have liked the idea. Before going to bed we jettisoned some more ashes into the Loire itself.

'Back in Paris we had two more important calls to make. First, the Palais de la Légion d'Honneur, where Sargent had received a wartime decoration (one of several, which included an award for foiling a plot to blow up General Eisenhower). We laid some ashes reverently under the portico of this imposing building, then hailed a taxi carrying our last portion of Sargent in the casket. The Bois de Boulogne, the huge park on the western side of Paris, is now rather seedy – the playground of pimps, whores and pederasts – compared to Sargent's day. But it was where he had spent much of his childhood. Sadly, there was nothing left of his address, which appeared to have been flattened by blocks of flats. We found a spot where the house might have been and buried the remaining ashes in a shallow grave. The casket itself we hung on to, brought back to the hotel, and carried with us in the taxi to our Eurostar train back to London.

'I placed it on the train table between us and settled down to watch the outskirts of Paris begin to race past our window. Then, for the first time, I noticed a label fastened to the bottom edge of the box. I had not bothered until now to look at the casket closely. I wiped away the film of ash that coated it. Then, my heart skipped a beat and I could hardly stifle a cry. Peter looked at me. "Oh my God!" I said. There could be no doubt. The label read: "Mrs Muriel Dodge." It was the wrong box.'

FLYING WITH SUPERMAN

Technique is what you fall back on
when you run out of inspiration.

Rudolf Nureyev

ONE MORNING IN EARLY 1982, I was flying by American Airlines from Los Angeles to New York on a publishing mission. My publishing company was doing well and I was flying first class. Arriving early, I settled comfortably into my wide light grey leather aisle seat. I had a lot of reading to do.

There was a pile of newspapers on the window seat next to me. I presumed that my travelling companion had come before me and wandered off elsewhere. However, shortly before take-off, an exotic-looking figure, dressed in baggy black Kireyeva trousers and a black silk Rubakha shirt buttoned at the neck, arrived. Before getting into his seat he asked in a thick Russian accent: 'Are these your papers?' I shook my head, whereupon the black-suited stranger picked up the newspapers and flung them into the aisle. He settled down, grabbed a flight magazine from the seat pouch in front of him, and flicked through the pages. I stole a glance at him and realized that my companion was none other than Rudolf Nureyev, the Soviet Union's most famous ballet dancer until he defected to the West. Neither of us said anything. He would have had no idea who I was, of course, and I was not about to tell him that I had recently been elected to the board of directors of the National Ballet of Canada, since I knew that Nureyev had just been dismissed from his position as a lead dancer by the Canadian ballet company. I fidgeted nervously.

Take-off was on time. Then the flight stewardess took our pre-lunch drinks orders. I had a single glass of champagne. Nureyev drank a large Bloody Mary, then another one, and yet another, in the hour or so before we were served lunch. We were given some strange seafood appetizer and both of us asked for and received a glass of white Burgundy. 'This food is awful!' said Nureyev. I agreed, and introduced myself. 'What are you doing with yourself now?' I ventured. 'I've been doing some film work in L.A.', replied Nureyev. 'But I'm hoping to go to the Paris Opera Ballet next year. They've asked me to be the director but it hasn't been approved yet. Right now I'm going to New York to do some television work.'

I was thrilled to be sitting next to Nureyev. He was a very easy conversationalist and happy to discuss his extraordinary life and career. I already knew quite a lot about him. I had read that he was born on a Trans-Siberian Railway train in 1939 and fell in love with ballet when his mother smuggled him into a performance of *Song of the Cranes* in Bashkiria. He was pushed into dancing Bashkir folk dances, and his enthusiastic and precocious attitude was soon apparent to his teachers, who urged him to study in Leningrad. Touring with a local ballet company he auditioned for the Bolshoi Ballet in Moscow and, surprisingly, was accepted. But, ever the individualist even at that young age, Nureyev spurned the Bolshoi and instead joined the Leningrad Choreographic School, an associate school of the famous Kirov Ballet. It was at the Kirov, after graduating, that Nureyev became a soloist. He soon became one of the Soviet Union's best-known dancers but was allowed to dance only within the country. Then in 1961 Nureyev was chosen to replace the Kirov's leading male dancer, who was injured, on their European tour. In Paris, his dancing electrified audiences but at the same time alarmed the Kirov's management and the KGB. They wanted to send him back to Russia because he was mixing with foreigners. They lied to him that his mother was seriously ill. But he knew that if he ever went back he would be arrested and would never be allowed to dance again. So, with little alternative, Nureyev defected at Paris airport, aided by the French police. Within less than a week he was dancing with the Grand Ballet du Marquis de Cuevas in *Sleeping Beauty* with Nina Vyroubova. Again he electrified audiences, toured with the company and, in Denmark, met the dancer Erik Bruhn who became his lover and mentor (and who would be appointed director of the National Ballet of Canada in 1983, where he would serve until his death). Nureyev was not allowed back into the Soviet Union for another twenty-eight years; in 1989 Mikhail Gorbachev permitted him to visit his dying mother.

Since 1961, Nureyev's fame as a dancer had become worldwide. He was first invited to dance in England by Dame Margot Fonteyn, the Royal Ballet's prima ballerina. He danced *Poème Tragique*, a solo, and the Black Swan *pas de deux* from *Swan Lake*. In 1962 he was invited by Dame Ninette de Valois to become a principal dancer with the Royal Ballet and for the first time he partnered Margot Fonteyn, in *Giselle*. Fonteyn and Nureyev became one of ballet's great partnerships, and were rumoured to have been lovers. *Marguerite and Armand* was their signature piece. Nureyev stayed with the Royal Ballet for another eight years, concentrating on a series of international guest appearances. In fact, he was still performing with the company when I met him, and he continued with them until he moved to the Paris Opera Ballet the following year. Amazingly, Margot Fonteyn went on dancing with him until the end of her sixth decade. Their last performance together was in *Baroque Pas de Trois* on 16 September 1988. Nureyev was then fifty years old.

Now here was I, sitting next to one of the world's great ballet dancers, having lunch, complaining about the food, and drinking too many glasses of chilled white Burgundy. Eventually, guiltily, I did tell him that I was on the board of the National Ballet of Canada. 'They got rid of me, you know,' he said sadly, 'but Erik is still there. He is very sick', which I also knew. We discussed everything, particularly Paris and the Paris Opera Ballet. Nureyev was having trouble with the French authorities getting a permanent work permit and had become an Austrian citizen. For some reason this helped matters in Paris.

We ate our chicken main course, drank more wine, had a chocolate mousse pudding and were still chatting and drinking coffee when the lights were dimmed and a large screen was lowered to show the feature film. It was *Superman*. Immediately, Nureyev became very serious and quiet. He grabbed his headphones, stopped talking and concentrated on the film. I followed suit, although I didn't think *Superman* was the kind of film I would normally be keen to see. But Nureyev was intent on watching Christopher Reeve as Superman, along with Gene Hackman, Margot Kidder, Marlon Brando, Glenn Ford and some other big names.

In case you don't know, *Superman* is the film widely credited with bringing science-fiction films and super-hero films back into Hollywood cinema. It shows the early years of Superman, the comic-strip character. As a small child, Kal-El, he is found by Jonathan and Martha Kent in Smallville, Kansas. They take the child home after seeing the toddler lift the rear-end of Jonathan's pick-up truck, thus saving Jonathan's life. They call him Clark and lovingly raise him as their own son. Fourteen years later, the teenager exhibits extraordinary powers: he can outrun speeding trains and kick a football into the stratosphere. As an adult, disguised as a newspaper reporter, Clark Kent conceals his prowess as he develops a romance with Lois Lane (Margot Kidder). But soon he is battling his arch-enemy, Lex Luthor, who plans to make a fortune in real estate by buying enormous tracts of cheap desert land and then diverting a nuclear rocket from a missile testing site to blow apart the San Andreas Fault. Although this plan will kill millions of people, and destroy California, it will make Luthor's real estate into the new west coast of America.

The plot is complicated, with many twists and turns. But of course there is endless scope to show Superman performing outrageous superhuman feats. The large-scale visual effects make for some astonishing sequences. It's a good story. Even better, though, was the extreme effect of the story on my new friend, Rudolf Nureyev.

He laughed, louder than any single person should in a confined space. Through my headphones I could hear his delighted screams. He kicked the seat in front of him, causing the woman occupying the seat to stand up and glare threateningly. He squirmed. He cackled. He stood up and applauded. He laughed and giggled again and again and again until, exhausted, at the end of the film Nureyev took off his earphones, put his head back, closed his eyes, and said: 'You Americans have the most incredible sense of humour.' And with that brief sentence, the great dancer sank into a deep sleep from which he did not wake until we were circling Kennedy Airport, about to land in New York.

GRAND SLAM

*Bridge is the most entertaining and intelligent
card game the wit of man has so far devised.*

W. Somerset Maugham,
Introduction to *The Standard Book of Bidding*
by Charles Goren, 1944

I AM THE FIRST to say that I have always been a very, very
mediocre bridge-player – whereas Zia Mahmood is undoubtedly one
of the greatest of bridge-players, if not *the* greatest in the world.
So there was zero possibility that I would ever find myself in the
position of playing against him, leave alone partnering him. Yet,
strangely enough, the latter is exactly what happened in 2002 when
my wife Valda, a member of the Andrew Robson Bridge Club in
London, and a regular player there, bought Zia Mahmood for £500
as my partner to play in a charity bridge tournament raising money
for cancer treatment.

At first I refused to play, insisting that Valda should partner the
great Zia. But in the end I was persuaded despite my reservations.
I set about learning everything I could concerning Zia, and also
learning some of the many bridge conventions. In fact, I took a
couple of lessons from Simon Stocken, a professional at the Andrew
Robson Bridge Club.

Zia Mahmood was born on 7 January 1946 in Karachi. He was
educated in England, qualified as a chartered accountant, and spent
three years running *Dawn*, his family's newspaper in Pakistan. Now

very much part of the London bridge scene, he is a grand master of both the World Bridge Federation and the American Contract Bridge League. He is known to have an amazing knack of bringing out the very best from his partners. But what on earth was he going to be able to get out of me? I was naturally terrified. And when I read his autobiography, *Bridge My Way*, I became even more terrified. How did his extraordinary mind work? Let me give you an example.

Zia recalls that early on in his career he was asked a tricky question: 'You are shown three doors and told there is a Rolls-Royce behind one of them and booby prizes behind the others. You choose one. Now the quizmaster, who knows where the Rolls is, must open one of the remaining two doors, behind one of which he knows is a booby prize. Then he offers you the chance to stay with the door or to change to the other unopened door. What should you do?'

Zia opts to change doors and explains why. 'The doors are called A, B and C. In each case we choose A. There are three possibilities:

1. The Rolls-Royce is indeed behind A. After we choose A, the Quizmaster opens B (or it could have been C which also has a booby prize behind the door) and offers us C. We accept and change our choice. We lose the Rolls-Royce.
2. The Rolls-Royce is behind B. The quizmaster opens C (he is not allowed to open B this time because the Rolls-Royce is there) and offers us B. We accept and win the Rolls-Royce.
3. The Rolls-Royce is behind C. The quizmaster opens B (he is not allowed to open C) and offers us C. We accept, changing our choice from A to C. We win the Rolls-Royce.'

Zia then concludes: 'As you can see, the odds are actually two to one to change doors. It didn't look like that at first; it is a kind of optical illusion. The argument is like the Principle of Restricted Choice in bridge.'

How could I conceivably keep up with this kind of thinking? It was way above me. Before the tournament I simply had to find a way to put myself on an even footing with Zia. This is what I decided.

When the day came, and the great Zia Mahmood arrived at Claridge's to play, he understandably asked me: 'What conventions do you play?' I immediately answered: 'No conventions!' Feigning satisfaction, he simply said: 'Much better. Much better.' He was the perfect gentleman. And then we settled down to play. Duplicate. Twenty-four hands.

Actually, we did quite well. Why shouldn't we, given Zia's mastery of the game. The trouble was, I was playing most of the hands, which was not at all what I had anticipated. Still, we came out in the top third in performance, among the thirty or forty teams playing.

Then, as the evening was drawing to a close and most of the players had finished their scheduled games, there were just a few matches still to play. We were one of them: Zia and I, versus two very experienced women opponents whose names I shall withhold, for reasons that will become obvious. I suppose that because we were one of the last teams to play, and the great Zia was there, a crowd of forty or fifty people gathered round our table to watch. I was desperately conscious of all the critical eyes upon us, and determined not to make a fool of myself.

Zia, the dealer, opened the bidding. Three No Trumps! My God, I thought, this is going to be exciting, because I had a very good hand. Nineteen points. Five good hearts: ace, king to the jack, ten and six; the ace, king and two small spades; a singleton diamond, the jack; and the queen, jack and a small club. Immediately, the lady to Zia's left (East) politely but firmly asked me: 'What does he mean by that bid?' This threw me for a moment, and I was more than aware of all the watching bridge-players who were going to hang on my every word. Then I replied: 'Either he's got twenty-one or twenty-two points; or he's got a long suit (at least seven I hoped); or he's really upset because I've been playing all the hands.' This provoked some nervous but polite laughter around the table. No more questions. I felt I had answered correctly. East passed. I responded with Four Hearts. A pause. Then the lady on my left (West) also passed. Zia went up to Five Hearts – and my spirits sank. I thought: Oh God, he's going to make *me* play this final hand, in front of all these experts who certainly want to see Zia play it, not me. East passed again. Now I became really determined to get Zia to play the hand. My thinking was this. There are only forty points in a pack of cards. I had nineteen of them. If Zia truly had twenty points, then there must be only one face card out there in the other two hands. So I gambled. I was damned if I was going to play the hand in hearts. I had therefore somehow got to get Zia out of hearts. I bid Six No Trumps – a reckless pre-emptive jump. Zia didn't turn a hair. He showed absolutely no expression. But there was a slight murmur in the crowd. It wasn't surprising. I was surprised at myself. West passed once more, so did Zia, and so did the lady on my right. Zia would have to play the hand in no trumps.

East led out the six of spades. Unfortunately for our opponents, but fortunately for us, she could not know that her partner had both the ace and king of clubs. If East had instead led a club, Zia and I would have been badly down. I laid out my hand as dummy and Zia took the spade trick with my ace. Then he methodically, without hesitation, took all twelve remaining tricks – a bravura performance. He never once led a club, and West's king and ace of clubs fell to Zia's last two diamonds. But while the cards were actually falling, I had been counting in my head. With horror I had realized that Zia, although he did have seven good diamonds, had only *nine* points in his hand – less than half of what I had expected. His opening bid of Three No Trumps had indeed been a gambler's bid. By sheer luck, our two hands had been a perfect fit, giving us a Grand Slam in front of this critical crowd.

There was even some enthusiastic clapping. For fifteen minutes, I was a hero. 'How did you know? How did you know?' Zia cried as he reached across the table to shake my hand. Of course, I didn't know. But he was so happy. I was happy too. Although we didn't win the tournament, my wife was thrilled, and so was Zia's wife Emma. The four of us had dinner together afterwards.

It was a magical evening, which I shall never forget. Since that day, I have not played another game of bridge. Why should I? I had had my time in the sun.

THE BLUE NUDE

*We are like sculptors, constantly carving out of
others the image we long for, need, love or desire,
often against reality, against their benefit, and
always, in the end, a disappointment, because it
does not fit them.*

Anaïs Nin,
The Diary of Anaïs Nin, VI, 1955–66

AMONG THE STRONGEST passions of my life is collecting. Like all
serious collectors, I have certain obsessions. One of them is knives of
all kinds, cultures and periods; another is the art of Ceylon and Sri
Lanka created during the twentieth century. Of all the remarkable
modern paintings from the island I have collected since I was in my
twenties, the one I love the most is *The Blue Nude*, painted in Paris
by Justin Daraniyagala. It hangs in the bedroom of my London flat,
opposite my bed. I find it difficult to imagine living without it.

It is seldom that a major Sri Lankan artist interconnects with
authors and artists of a different world and culture – but that is what
happened in an extraordinary encounter in Paris in the late 1920s.
Justin Daraniyagala was born in Ceylon in 1903 and received his early
art education at the Mudaliyar Amerasekera's Art School in
Colombo. After studies at Trinity College, Cambridge, from 1922 to
1927, where he obtained a law degree and also a 'blue' for boxing in
the bantam-weight class, he was encouraged by the artist Augustus
John to study painting at the Slade School of Art in London, which
he did in 1926–27. It was at the Slade that he won his first prize for

drawing. In 1928 he joined the Académie Julian in Paris and there, during the years 1928 and 1929, he met and worked with Henri Matisse and Pablo Picasso, both of whom influenced his work.

It was in Paris too, during those years, that he met the writer Anaïs Nin, who had started keeping her famous diary in 1914, when she was only eleven years old. Eventually, the diary comprised 35,000 handwritten pages, constantly revised to conform to her ever-changing view of those whom she had allowed into her life.

Nin was then married to an American banker, Hugh Guiler, and she remained married to him for the rest of her life. But in 1931 she began an affair with the writer Henry Miller, author of *Tropic of Cancer* and *Tropic of Capricorn*. She deceived her long-suffering and tolerant husband with Henry Miller, then Miller with her psychiatrist, as well as several of their friends. Finally Joaquin Nin, her pianist father, came back into her life. In 'Incest', part of *A Journal of Love: The Unexpurgated Diary of Anaïs Nin* (1932–34), she explains how, twenty years earlier, her father had abandoned her and her mother in New York. Then she gives details of how she seduced her father. This was also the covert theme of her *House of Incest* – a book much admired in the 1940s by the American critic Edmund Wilson and by Gore Vidal, the author of *Palimpsest*. Eventually, at the outbreak of the Second World War in 1939, Miller retreated to the safer shores of California, while Nin and her husband returned to New York. There she embarked on a now-legendary career promoting the existence of her extraordinary diaries, which Henry Miller greeted as a celebration of her life and loves.

However, back in 1928–29, before she met Miller, Anaïs Nin, always searching for love, and for a publisher for her diary, and forever short of money, resorted to posing nude for a number of artists, including Matisse, Picasso and Daraniyagala.

In 'Artists and Models', an excerpt from her much later erotic collection *Delta of Venus*, Nin described the experience of posing:

One morning I was called to a studio where a sculptor was beginning a statuette. He already had a rough version of the figure he wanted and had reached the stage where he wanted a model. The statuette was wearing a clinging dress, and the body showed through in every line and curve. The sculptor asked me to undress completely because he could not work otherwise. He seemed so absorbed by the statuette and looked at me so absently that I was able to undress and take the pose without hesitation. Although I was quite innocent at the time, he made me feel as if my body was no different than my face, as if I were the same as the statuette. Whenever I left the sculptor's studio I would always stop in the coffee shop nearby and ponder all that he had told me . . . I began to love posing for the adventurous aspect of it.

Gore Vidal describes how he saw Nin in those early Paris days. 'Tweezed eyebrows in the twenties manner. Beautiful hazel eyes . . . The body was that of a dancer, very slender, with a long waist, small breasts with pink nipples – like a girl.' In return she called Vidal 'a nice little monster I have taken to my breast'.

The Blue Nude, Daraniyagala's painting of Anaïs Nin, recalls Picasso's statement that 'a painting is the sum of its destructions'. Justin Daraniyagala was never content with an image, forever correcting and changing; discovering new states and forms; using palette-knives, brushes, and even his fingers to create a revealing emotional expression behind which one can detect ghosts of experience. It is in grasping this expression that one discovers his genius. In the words of a Sri Lankan art critic, S. B. Dissenayake, 'dense layers of hesitation and ambiguities preponderate. In the images he created he externalised and visualised his inner world. Rhythms and patterns arose not in relation to the image, but independently, while the image itself emerged unwilled as it were out of a dance of line and colour across the picture surface.' For me, *The Blue Nude* bursts with life and a very special kind of lyricism.

Although Nin never mentions Daraniyagala by name in her published diaries, one is compelled to wonder what effect this slim dusky aristocrat from Ceylon had on the ambitious and sensuous young author. Daraniyagala must have cut an incongruous figure in the bohemian Paris of the 1920s – totally unlike the boisterous Picasso and the quiet Matisse. He and his model were the same age – barely twenty-six years old. He wealthy, she poor; he single, she already married to her banker-protector. Whatever their relationship may have been, perhaps merely the fleeting encounter of an artist and model, Daraniyagala's *Blue Nude* is the only known portrait of the young Anaïs Nin. He himself loved the painting and took it with him when he returned to Ceylon in 1929 to his imposing family house in Nugedola, Pasyala, where it hung in the main drawing room together with sketches by Augustus John, Matisse and Modigliani, surrounded by a rare collection of South Indian bronzes and Chinese jade vases. He refused to sell the painting, and it was still with him when he died in 1967. After that, I bought it from his family and brought it back to Europe, where I have hardly ever allowed it out of my sight.

MEISNER'S ISLAND

No man is an Island, entire of it self; every man
is a piece of the Continent, a part of the main ...
And therefore never send to know for whom the
bell tolls; it tolls for thee.

John Donne,
'Meditation XVII',
Devotions upon Emergent Occasions, 1624

IT WAS A VERY HOT SUMMER in Nova Scotia – that summer of 2010. When we arrived on the island in the middle of July, a heat wave was in progress. The thermometer went higher than I have ever known it, and I've been going to Chester for over thirty-five years.

The island is a remarkable place. It covers a hundred acres just off Chester's Front Harbour on Mahone Bay, which got caught up in the war between the young United States of America and Great Britain two centuries ago. On 27 June 1813, the schooner-rigged American privateer *Teazer* was chased into Mahone Bay by the *Sir John Sherbrook* and was about to be captured when one of her crew members apparently threw a burning coal into the *Teazer*'s powder magazine. Only seven out of the thirty-seven American crew survived. The remains of the ship were towed into Chester and then beached on the island. The hull was sold and used as the foundation for what is now the Rope Loft Restaurant on the mainland, while part of the keel became the wooden cross in St Stephen's Church. Twelve bodies were taken from the ship to a house on the Front Harbour, but the following morning, before the burial in the town cemetery, only eleven bodies were found. They say that house is still haunted. Sometimes on 27 June, though not every year, a strange blue fire can be seen from the mainland on the horizon at almost the exact spot where the *Teazer* was blown to smithereens.

In those days, the island was called Norse Island. Today, it is known as Meisner's Island, named by a family who owned it and lived there for many years. My wife and I bought Meisner's Island after I dreamed that the island was for sale, twenty years ago. We go there every summer, as do our children and grandchildren, coming from Devon and West Sussex in England, Los Angeles and Connecticut in the United States. Over time, we have cleared away the dead spruce trees, created fields of grass on the three low rounded hills that surround the freshwater lake, and allowed new spruce and birch to come up so as to create a paradise. We are away from intruders there – or so we thought until the unexpected events of that summer.

Unknowingly, we had created a wildlife sanctuary for herons, owls, marsh hawks, ospreys, bald eagles, Canada geese, as well as mink, the occasional sea otter, and white-tailed deer. It was our clover that attracted the deer. We had planted it to make the fields look green before the grass grew. The deer caught the scent of the clover from the mainland and swam over for a meal. Soon, they settled on the island. We got used to them coming out of the elder and wild rose bushes in the early morning and at dusk, but they never ventured close to the main lodge where we live. Gradually they became tamer, and we could sometimes walk to within ten feet or so of the does and their fawns. The fawns were born in the early spring on the island, because the place was so safe. There were young stags, too. They could be quite aggressive, sparring with each other almost as soon as their young horns appeared. They made a wonderful sight against the red sunset sky.

With the extraordinary heat that summer, the deer seemed to have a hard time getting enough food. It did not rain much, and there was not as much of the young grass that the deer love. So, over the summer, the deer – particularly the young stags – grew bolder and bolder, and came closer and closer to the main lodge, where my wife has created a small vegetable garden, much protected and appreciated by our grandchildren. Now, when we opened the back door that leads out next to the vegetable garden, the deer stood their ground, unafraid of our human presence. The young stags stamped their feet at our unwanted intrusion on what was fast becoming their territory. But eventually they still scampered away to safety and we thought nothing more about their unusual behaviour.

Then, one Friday evening in late August, after our children and grandchildren had left, we returned to the island by boat after having drinks on the Chester peninsula with a few friends. Driving over the hill to the main lodge, we were flabbergasted to see as many as eighteen or twenty white-tailed deer in the large field that sweeps down to the lodge. Moreover, two of the larger stags, as well as a few does, had positioned themselves right in front of the back door almost in a semicircle across the path. We drove up cautiously to avoid frightening the animals. But we needn't have worried. Far from being frightened, they seemed fearless and stepped towards our jeep. Eventually, we had to use the vehicle as a sort of battering ram to push the stags away from the back door and make our way into the lodge.

It was unknown behaviour, at any rate in Nova Scotia. We had heard of recent attacks by male deer in California. In fact, Californian wildlife officials had warned people to keep their distance from the animals. But we never expected this to happen to us, and certainly not on Meisner's Island. In California, the attacks seemed to be the result of residential areas expanding into the countryside, so that wild deer were becoming less afraid of humans. We heard of an elderly man being attacked by a stag as he was picking tomatoes in his garden. He was gored in the face, rushed to hospital where he received two hundred and twenty stitches, but died three weeks later from a pulmonary blood clot. There was a second report of a couple in California attacked while watering a friend's vegetable garden. The woman was gored in the arm after the animal pinned her husband to the ground with its antlers. When the woman tried to scare it off with a piece of plywood, she was gored again. Several dogs had been killed.

What was going on? We knew, of course, that all deer can be dangerous in the rutting season. But not in August: the season for rutting is not until well into October and November. At that time the bucks focus on mating and wander for weeks looking for females, often not eating. They are expected to be aggressive then.

Two nights later – I remember there was a full moon – we were woken about two in the morning by a banging on what we thought was the back door. It became really persistent. We got out of bed. Looking out from our upstairs bedroom window we saw, on the moonlit ground at the side of the lodge, a herd of deer with two young stags and another somewhat bigger one. The stags were not just rubbing their antlers against the side of the house. Although it did not seem believable, it struck us that the stags were trying to enter the lodge.

We were alone on the island, and unarmed. We waited for another half hour. But the banging and knocking continued. Were the animals really trying to enter? Although we were not scared, we had no idea what to do. So – I'll admit in some desperation and despite the lateness of the hour – I telephoned Jimmy Refuse, who looks after Meisner's Island when we are away. I explained the peculiar situation.

It took him a while to surface from sleep. When he had, he didn't believe what I was telling him. 'OK,' he finally said, 'but I'm out on the Windsor Road and it'll take me at least half an hour to get to you.'

'You'd better bring your gun, Jim', I added. 'This looks a bit serious. And bring the tractor from the boathouse when you get to the island. I don't think I'll be able to get to the jeep from the lodge to pick you up.'

'I don't have any lights on the tractor,' he replied, 'but I'll bring the light from the boat.'

Jimmy arrived at the main lodge on Meisner's Island about forty-five minutes later, driving the island tractor, in the semi-darkness, armed with a searchlight and his 12-bore shotgun. The deer were still hanging around the back door, and two of the stags were still rattling away at the wooden siding, quite intent (so we thought) on breaking in. The noise of the tractor engine did nothing to deter them. Then, near the house, sitting on the tractor, Jimmy fired two shots away from the house into the air above the heads of the deer. Immediately they dispersed, including the stags, scampering over the nearby sloping ground to the protection of the dense elder thickets. It was an amazing sight. Jimmy Refuse said he had never seen anything like it in all the years he had lived in Chester.

We sat for a while in the narrow dining room below our bedroom looking south over the moonlit waters towards Tancook Island. The three of us were virtually speechless. What could we say? Then Jimmy mentioned something about stags in Wisconsin attacking a tavern and my ears pricked up. 'Now that I'm thinking,' he continued, 'I remember hearing about some deer, stags, that crashed through the front door of a pub in Menomonie in Wisconsin and knocked it right off its hinges. Nobody understood then why they did it. Caused quite a stir. People running all over the place in every direction. One stag actually ran through the bar area and got into the restaurant. They were big animals too – 150 to 175 pounds. Strangely, no one was hurt and the animals escaped into the woods nearby. But there was no explaining their behaviour – that is, until later. A game warden, called to the scene, speculated that one or both of the stags might have seen their reflection in one of the windows of the pub building, or perhaps in one of the panes of glass in the door. Maybe that would explain why they attacked what they thought was a rival beast.'

This set us thinking. There were all kinds of cuts and gouges in the wooden frame around the back door. We had glass panes in it. Perhaps the stags, disoriented by the freakishly hot weather and emboldened by the dearth of their usual food, had become confused by their reflections in the glass. This seemed at least possible, and would account for why they had never attacked the lodge before. But we were not entirely convinced. The animals' behaviour was really strange and unsettling.

Still, we had to let Jimmy go back to bed. He said his goodbyes, climbed back onto the tractor, and headed back over the hill to the boat dock on the other side of the island. We watched him drive away up the moonlit path – leaving us alone again on the island, with the deer.

THE GLENTHORNE CAT

...a dark shape some five foot long, crouched over the top of a hedge, green eyes glaring at the truck which dared to be in its way. The driver moved back up the slope to get a better look, but the animal disappeared in the shadows. It was May 2002 and it was the latest sighting of the Beast of Exmoor.

From a report in *Country Life* magazine,
September 2002

EXMOOR, WHERE I LIVE, is one of the smallest of England's national parks. Its total area is a mere 160,000 acres, or about 265 square miles. One third of the park lies in Devon, and two thirds in Somerset; its northern boundary is the southern coast of the Bristol Channel stretching from Combe Martin in the west to Minehead in the east. It is a wild expanse of moor, woods and heather, the lower slopes of which are covered with a chequered pattern of green fields in a medley of soft tones and colours. The sweep of the hills down to the sea in the north and their light tones contrast sharply with the deep green of the combes. All this is punctuated by small, tasteful, pink sandstone houses, the odd church and carefully tended colourful gardens.

But for all that Exmoor may lack in size, it more than makes up for in legends and superstitions. I used to hear about them, when I was a schoolboy at Blundell's in the 1940s, from my uncle, the Reverend David Cockle, who at that time was the vicar of Timberscombe, a tiny village in Somerset almost in the north corner of Exmoor. E. W. Hendy, author of *Wild Exmoor*, tells of many local beliefs. A black slug smeared on a wart and then placed on a thorn will rid you of the nasty growth. A sty can be treated if a woman passes her wedding ring over it four times from right to left. You can always tell the number of years before you will be married by hanging a sheep's heart in your house and counting the drops of blood that drip from it. Never burn old love letters . . . it is unlucky. If a door refuses to remain closed, this is a warning of imminent death. Keep a donkey among your cows to drive off witches. You can also keep a witch away by driving a nail into her footprint.

So perhaps it is not too surprising that in our own time considerable credence has been given to the so-called Beast of Exmoor. The first rumours of its existence started in the late 1970s. They reached a high in 1983, when eighty sheep on Exmoor were found dead by a farmer, their throats ripped out and their skin torn by claw marks. Farmers in the area reported sightings of large cat-like creatures with black or dark grey fur, a long tail and green eyes, which stood low to the ground. The reports mushroomed and were taken so seriously that in 1988 the then Ministry of Agriculture, Fisheries and Food sent a party of Royal Marines to carry out a search, and if possible shoot the creature with a sniper's bullet. Although nothing was found, sightings persisted from time to time, as late as 2002. I personally can vouch for having seen claw marks about six feet above the ground on trees abutting the coastal path above and west of my house at Glenthorne, similar to the territorial markings made by a large cat, probably a leopard.

Glenthorne is about half-way along the northern boundary of Exmoor, not far from Countisbury. It occupies the only piece of flat land between Porlock and Lynmouth, at the end of a three-mile drive said to be the longest in England, which zigzags and drops 1,088 feet down over a hog's back from County Gate to a grassy clearing in a combe, where the house was built in 1830. The northern edge of our lawn is a cliff that falls 150 feet into the sea. Woods behind the house climb steep hills that are occasionally separated by narrow streams hidden by fern and rhododendrons, which tumble over mossy rocks down to the stony beach. There are old smugglers' paths all around, one of which tracks a stream down to a waterfall that cascades into the sea. It was from this beach that the materials to build Glenthorne were brought by boat by the Reverend Walter S. Halliday, a reclusive clergyman who fell in love with the magnificent situation.

I had heard about Glenthorne from my clergyman uncle while I was at Blundell's, but had never visited the house at the bottom of the dirt track leading down from the moors. I knew that it had always been in the possession of the Halliday family. There were less reliable stories about it, too. Some people who had ventured there uninvited had supposedly never come back. The house was said to be haunted by the Reverend Halliday's ghost.

Then in 1984, on my first visit to my old school in twenty-eight years, I heard that Glenthorne was for sale. I was warned that the house was virtually in ruins, but this did not dissuade me, and eventually my wife agreed. With very little hesitation I hired a lawyer in nearby Minehead and we paid the asking price for the ruined building. Over the next few years, while continuing to live in Canada, my wife and I painstakingly restored Glenthorne according to an early Victorian print of the house, which we found in an antique shop in Lynton. We repaired the Delabole slate roof, the Gothic spires and the broken Bath stone balustrades and we returned the many rooms and corridors of the building to their original pre-Victorian prime, as near as we could establish from studying its history. We paid particular attention to the magnificent library added in 1846 on the ground floor, and the first-floor study of the Reverend Halliday, who was a quintessential bibliophile. At last, in 1988, disillusioned with the North American financial scene with its ever-growing responsibilities, we sold our house in Toronto, moved into a flat on Sloane Square in London, and determined to spend more time at Glenthorne.

It is an enigmatic place, and we always felt, as we still do today, that even though we legally owned Glenthorne, in reality the house remained the domain of its creator. The Reverend Halliday died in 1872, yet we felt that he was always watching us. When we hung some old hunting prints in the back hall, near the kitchen (all built by the reverend), one obviously unacceptable hunting scene was literally thrown across the hall and the substantial nail which we had hammered into the wall was bent double. We hung the old print in a less conspicuous place. When we installed a radio and tape-player in the downstairs library, the panelled door to the room with its rounded corners, walled with books, banged constantly for nearly ten minutes – to the amazement of the engineer. On this occasion, we left the small radio–tape-player in place, hidden between leather-bound books, and had no further trouble.

The reverend seemed to be around mostly at night or in the early hours of the morning, and usually in his study on the first floor, looking out over the old croquet lawn eastwards down the steep cliffs to the Bristol Channel. We often heard him but we never saw him.

That is, until that one cold December night in 2004, soon after I returned to Glenthorne from a research visit to Sri Lanka. I was now battling with the manuscript that became *Woolf in Ceylon*, tracing the seven years that Leonard Woolf spent in Ceylon from 1904 to 1911 as a young British civil servant, just before he returned to England, wrote his powerful novel *A Village in the Jungle*, and then married Virginia. My goal was to discuss not only Woolf's career in Ceylon but also its significance to the history of Ceylon after he left, particularly after independence in 1948. Empire, with all its fascinating contradictions that Woolf and I had personally experienced, was on my mind, and I suppose my thoughts and imagination were racing. In truth, I felt overwhelmed by the task I had set myself.

It was very late and my wife had already gone to bed. I settled down in my favourite armchair, closed my eyes for a moment, and suddenly I realized that there was someone else in the room. The feeling was not at all frightening; far from it. It was quite reassuring. When I opened my eyes, I saw an old gentleman well wrapped up in a scarf and nightgown, seated in a chair (not one of mine) a short distance away from me. He was looking at me quizzically. I had no idea what to do or say, but I was quite relaxed. It was obvious – not least from an old portrait painting I had seen – that I was at long last in the presence of the Reverend Halliday.

'I see that you're writing a book about Ceylon.' His voice was low, but quite audible.

'I am, Sir,' I replied, 'and I'm not having an easy time of it.'

There was a pause. The reverend seemed to be looking me up and down and thinking about whether or not to say more. I was anxious that he would simply vanish, but the old man seemed to be quite comfortable and intent on having a conversation.

'You know,' he said after the short silence, 'you're not the first person from Ceylon to have lived or stayed at Glenthorne.'

'I know, Sir. I have been told that Samuel Baker, who spent some years in Ceylon, used to come down here in the early 1870s after his discovery of Lake Albert.'

'Yes. That's certainly true. He was an interesting man and became something of a friend. He came to stay with his Hungarian wife several times. Full of stories and adventures. She was quite a woman. He bought her out of a slave market in Turkey and she stuck with him through all his adventures on the Nile. But I am not referring to Baker.'

I was now hugely curious. The reverend continued: 'Do you know that a friend of my family, actually a friend of my favourite nephew, also went out to Ceylon and lived there for a while? Then he came back to England and lived here at Glenthorne. I say that he lived here, and he did, but only for a few months, because he got involved in a strange situation.'

The reverend startled me with his next question. 'What do you know about the cat people of Ceylon?'

I was disconcerted. Although I have always been intrigued by mythology, witchcraft and superstition, I had never seriously thought about cat people in connection with Ceylon. Fortunately, I had just been reading up on the early history of Ceylon, and its village superstitions, in order to write about Leonard Woolf and his novel. I replied: 'Well, Sir, I do know that the beginnings of Ceylon remain in the realm of fantasy, but of course I don't know whether the myths are really true. The story in the *Mahavansa*, the epic of the Sinhalese, is that there was a king of the Indian city of Sinhapura who was the result of a princess mating with a lion, a *sinha*. This king then produced a son, Vijaya, but he banished this prince for his riotous ways and sent him into exile with his rowdy companions in a rudderless boat. Somehow, the boat arrived at the island of what is now known as Sri Lanka. Am I on the right track?'

'Possibly. What else do you know?'

'Well, some people maintain that Sinhapura was in Bengal. But I do not agree, because the only lions in India are found in the Gir forest of Gujarat on the west coast. Furthermore, there is a fishing village called Sinhapura below the Rann of Kutch. This suggests that Gujarat is more likely to be the birthplace of the prince.'

'Go on', the reverend encouraged me.

'Prince Vijaya took a local enchantress, Kuveni, for his mistress and she gave birth to two children. Thus Vijaya became the founder of the Sinhalese race. When he discarded Kuveni, she turned into a leopard in order to avenge herself on Vijaya.' At this point, I hesitated: were I to have continued I would have had to admit there was not much more that I knew about cat people and Ceylon.

After a reasonably polite silence, the old man continued. His voice was now a little hard to catch, as he related an amazing story about Glenthorne and Ceylon, barely stopping, though sometimes faltering with emotion.

'As I told you, my nephew's friend spent some time in Ceylon. He worked in Colombo but also up-country on the Glencairn tea estate – a place called Bogawantalawa. You have probably been there. He was very taken by the country and by the people, particularly the Sinhalese. He became very friendly with a Sinhalese family of aristocratic Kandyan origin who were neighbours of his on the Glencairn estate, and he fell in love with the daughter. Kumari was her name. Despite considerable objection from his family, he married her in a secret Buddhist ceremony and brought her back to England less than six months later to live here at Glenthorne. By then, he had fallen out with his own people in England. We didn't know it, but almost from the outset the marriage had run into trouble. Despite the obvious love of the young couple, my nephew and I could see that the two of them were far from complementary. Not even my nephew had any idea what the real problem was. We had to go to great lengths in order to keep the relationship a secret. There are no near neighbours at Glenthorne, as you know, but we had visitors from time to time. At any rate, only the immediate family was allowed to know that our guest had brought back a dark wife from Ceylon. Finally, however, the situation became too much to bear even for the young man. One night, actually in this very room, he came to me in a terrible state and broke down. He told me that despite their great love, the marriage had never been consummated.'

I must admit that I had been half expecting this explanation – not least because the same was true of Leonard and Virginia Woolf's marriage. But what came next from the reverend was beyond my wildest imaginings. He appeared almost at a loss for words, and on the point of breaking down himself. As he explained it, he had tried to reason with the young man, but no reasoning was possible. For the truth appeared to be too incredible for rational arguments. Here, at Glenthorne, Kumari had confessed to her young husband of an over-weening anxiety. As the direct descendant of an aristocratic family whose ancestors sprang from the relationship between a human being and a cat, she feared that if she allowed herself to become sexually aroused by a man, she would be transformed into a lion or a leopard.

Both of us were now silent. I could think of nothing to say. I might have relished such a tall tale if told to me in Sri Lanka, India, or some other eastern country, but here I was, in the heart of England, hearing the story from a long-dead English clergyman. Why was he telling me this? And why now? Did he have any evidence that the fantastic story was true?

The Reverend Halliday seemed in no particular hurry to continue. He looked at me searchingly. I was glued to his eyes for fear of break-ing the spell. But I didn't dare to ask: 'What happened next?' At long last, he spoke again.

'There was nothing I could do to console my young friend. We talked into the night. I assured him that tales of the supernatural were seldom true. There was certainly no scientific evidence for the transformation of people into lions or leopards, despite all the myths. All I could advise was that he should give his bride all the affection and comfort she so obviously craved. In time, I said, I had faith that her fears would be overcome, and the two of them would live a normal and happy married life. And I really believed this was true.

'For the next few weeks the strained situation continued. But nothing more was said and the young man did not try to discuss his wife with me again. As we had no visitors, the young couple came down to meals together as usual, walked hand in hand around the gardens, and sometimes followed the smugglers' paths onto the heights of Exmoor. If one did not know the awful truth, one would have suspected nothing from their outward appearance. I began to feel more relaxed.

'However, I have always found that one feels most secure just before a storm. And so it was that one summer night in July I was awakened some time after midnight by my young friend in a state of great agitation.

'"She's gone," he told me.

'"What do you mean?" I asked, not wanting to believe him.

'"Something strange happened. We were asleep in our bedroom down the hall from yours; and then quite suddenly I woke up in Kumari's arms. She had been crying. I could taste the tears on her cheek. But she clung to me as if her very life depended on it. I must say that at that moment I loved her totally. We held each other close, neither one of us wanting to release the other. I wanted her terribly, but did not dare to make a move, knowing her irrational fear. Yet, somehow she seemed released of her strange belief, free and different, almost happy – the passionate lover I always desired and hoped she would be. I knew she wanted me as I wanted her. Her breathing became faster. I felt her body arch and quiver and her head force itself under mine. Her naked passion appeared to have no boundaries. Then, writhing beneath me, she suddenly screamed, still gripping me tightly: 'No. No. Not yet.' She broke away from me, almost violently, and was gone. I couldn't see her, I couldn't stop her. I've been outside searching the bushes around the house, and walked the length of the water garden. The moon is almost full – but I saw nothing. Nothing. It's a warm night, but she has no clothes on and I'm afraid she'll catch her death of cold."

'What on earth was I to do?' the reverend asked, almost as if speaking to himself. 'I could not keep this quiet any longer. I summoned all the servants including the housemaid and together we lit lanterns and searched the grounds and some of the nearby paths almost until dawn. Eventually, I came back here and sank into this chair until the morning broke.'

'Did you find her?' I could not stop myself from asking.

'All we found was a broken window in the front hall which in our haste to get outside we had completely missed the night before. The panes had been shattered, and there were scratch marks and blood on the sill and on the frame. Outside the window on the dry soil were marks that seemed to have been made by some large cat-like animal – pug marks. We tried to follow them but only saw faint traces that some animal had made away from the house and up into the beech wood above the road. Then I had to break this news to my young friend. Of course, I also reported the missing person to the Countisbury constabulary, who organized search parties in the hills and woods around and behind Glenthorne, and also in the combes leading to Yenworthy and the valleys leading from the old Roman barrow near the coastal road. Apart from the broken window, nothing whatsoever turned up. After giving up all hope, my nephew's friend left Glenthorne and went back to his family in Yorkshire.

'So there is something for you to write about', the old man concluded companionably. I looked down for a moment, horrified but thrilled by his story. It made me want to tell him immediately of the claw marks I had observed on the trees near his house. But when I looked up, the Reverend Halliday was no longer there.